THE STORY OF IRISH DANCE

The Story of Irish Dance

Helen Brennan

ROBERTS RINEHART PUBLISHERS
Lanham, Maryland

Published in the United States and Canada
by Roberts Rinehart Publishers
An Imprint of The Rowman & Littlefield Publishing Group
4720 Boston Way
Lanham, MD 20706

Distributed by National Book Network

ISBN 1-58979-003-0 (paperback : alk. paper)
Library of Congress Control Number: 2001093519

Cover Design: Public Communications Centre, Dublin
Typesetting: Red Barn Publishing, Skeagh, Skibbereen

∞™ The paper used in this publication meets the minimum requirements of
American National Standard for Information Sciences—Permanence of
Paper for Printed Library Materials, ANSI/NISO Z39.48–1992.
Manufactured in the United States of America.

Dedication

This book is dedicated to all the dancers of Ireland, wherever they may be, and, most importantly, to the memory of my grandfather, Jim Brennan (Seumas Ó Braonáin), (1881–1970), Gaelic Leaguer, dancer, all-Ireland footballer and lover of language. *Duine uasal; calma, bríomhar, cróga*; who first put my foot on the road.

Acknowledgements

The following dancers personally provided me with material for this book, and their energy and enthusiasm were a constant source of inspiration:

Harry Fairtclough, Catherine Prendergast Fairtclough, Molly Rafferty, Jem Darby, Brigid Flanagan Howard, Annie May Fahy, Jenny Fahy Campbell, Josie McCormack Conway, Tony McNulty, Joe O'Donovan, Siobhán O'Donovan, Dan Furey, James Keane, Emer, Ciara and Michele McCarthy, Elaine McNamara, Vera Nugent, Rita Connell, Dan Keefe, "Pa" Keane, Dan Connell, Ger Collins, Abby Moynihan, Andy Sullivan, Connie Maic Tom, Willie Connell, Ger Milligan, Dan Keeffe, Eileen Buckley, Aileen Connell, Mary Clarke Carmody, Bill Kellegher, Siobhán Connell, Dan Joe Cahill, Kathleen Murphy, Jack Reen, Evelyn Cronin, Timmy Dineen, Eileen Courtney, Dan Scannell, Gracie O' Sullivan, Michael Leader, Mary Cronin, Dinny Cahill, Tony Shannon, Richard Leader, Timothy Moynihan, Nora O' Connor, Christy Kelly, Johnny Smith, Tom King, Michael Sexton, Kathleen King, Collette Carroll, Tom Hughes, Helen Caffrey, Geraldine Carroll, Pee Sexton, Anne Marie McInerney, Elizabeth King, Ultan Coleman, Teesie Blake, Judith McQuaid, Kathleen Brady, P.J. Carroll, Caroline Clarke, Pat Tierney, Marie Tierney, Pauline Tierney, Annette Tierney, Jim Halpin, Vincent Duffy, Peter Duffy, Johnny Magee, Paddy Magee, Ben (Sketch) McGrath, Philip Keown, Rose Johnston, Susie Keown, Jimmy Fehilly, Breandán (Bonnar) Ó Cnáimhsí, Séamus (Jimmy Mhary Whillie) Ó Dúgáin, Éamonn (Éamonn Mháire) Mac Ruairí, Margaret McHugh, Kitty McFadden, Siobhán Gallagher, Hugh Murphy, Artie Graham, Peter Duffy, Packy McAney, Jimmo Sexton, Jimmy Quinn, John Joe Moroney, Tom Queally, Baby Queally, Michael Currucane, Ollie Conway, Marie Conway, Paddy Neylon, Nellie Casey Cox, Tom Synan, Joan Murphy Looney, Maureen Johnston O'Loughlin, Cissie Crehan, Nell Gleeson, Anne Johnston Cavey, Martie Malley, Anthony (Tone) Darcy, Máire Mooney, Kitty Mooney, Anne Cunningham, Teresa Seán Cunningham, Mairéad Ní Mhaonaigh, Michael (Mickle) Quinn, Máirtín MacDonnacha, Máirtín Jaimsie Ó Flaithearta, Cóilín Dharach Seoighe, Colm (Sonny) Ó Méalóid, Annie Ní Dhúbháin, Mary Kemp Keating, Mike Dyer, Tommy Killoran, Kathleen McCoy, Rita Mulligan, Jim Corcoran, Davy Grady, Joe Ward, Paidí Bán Ó Broin.

Special thanks to:

An Comhairle Ealaíonn, The Arts Council of Northern Ireland, Ciarán Carson, Thady Casey, Willie Clancy, Jimmy Ward, J.C. Talty, Breandán Breathnach, Muiris Ó Rócháin, Ríonach Uí Ógáin and the staff of the Department of Irish Folklore, U.C.D., Harry Hughes, Micheál Ó Súilleabháin of the University of Limerick, Lillis Ó Laoire, do., Finbar Boyle; my aunt, Gráinne Brennan, Jim and Maggie McGrath, Tom King, Annie May Fahy, Mick Hoy, Mary MacConnell, Breandán (Bonnar) Ó Cnáimhsí, Joe and Siobhán O'Donovan, Donncha Ó hEallaithe, Proinsias Ó Maonaigh, Harry and Catherine Fairtclough, Brigid Flanagan Howard, Bob Quinn, Nicholas Carolan and the staff of I.T.M.A., Paddy O'Neill, Seán Ó Cearnaigh of the Ordnance Survey, Ireland; Proinsias Ó Conluain, Seamus Hosey, Martin Talty, Martin (Junior) Crehan, Seamus Tansey, the Irish Folklore Commission's collectors – in particular P. J. Gaynor, Jim Delaney, Michael J. Murphy, Seosamh Ó Dálaigh (Joe Daly), Séamus Ennis, Peadar Ó Discín and Nioclás Breathnach; Ted McGowan, Johnny O' Leary, Collette Conaghan, Joan Flett; Mothers Annunciata, Vianney and Gerard, who taught me English, Irish and Music in Loreto Convent, Bray; Michael (Mickle) Quinn, Seán Ó Cuinn of Tí Chúláin, Adrienne Kaeppler of the Smithsonian Institution, U.S.A.; Jean Jarrell of the Laban Centre, London; Tommy and Annette Munnelly, Pat O' Connell and Máire Delaney, Nuala O'Faoláin; my parents – Flann and Elsie Brennan née Hickey, my parents-in-law – Terry and Moira Corcoran née Quigley, Nuala O'Connor, Gary Matthews, Anne Kirwan-Kelly, Hae Kyung Um, Tomás Ó Faircheallaigh of An Coimisiún le Rincí Gaelacha, John Cullinane, do., Martin Stokes, formerly of Queen's University, Belfast, who constantly urged me to put my thoughts down on paper; and most especially my partner-in-life, Seán Corcoran, without whose love, support, clear-eyed insights and generosity of intellect this book would not have seen the light of day.

Contents

Introduction

THE JOURNEY WHICH led to this book begins in the mid-1950s in a draughty hall near the river in Athenry, County Galway, where a gaggle of little girls are being put through their dance paces by Miss Annie May Fahy of Tuam. "Up and back and one, two, three, four. Tap out one, tap out two, tap out three and four. Tap out one, tap out two, tap out three and four. Up and back and one, two, three, four." That is how she taught us the lead around or opening step of the double jig. We chanted as we danced and I, in my nine-year-old innocence, thought that all dance teachers did the same. That it was effective as a memory aid was evident some fourteen years later when I danced one of Miss Fahy's jig steps on the shining flag floor of Willie Clancy's kitchen in Miltown Malbay, County Clare. Willie was, of course, best known as one of Ireland's leading pipers, but in common with many people in the locality, he had, in his youth, learnt dancing from Thady Casey, a renowned local dancing master. "Do that one again, Helen," said Willie. "It's a grand step." As I beat out the rhythm with the mnemonic echoing in my head, I knew by Willie's interest that he might agree to teach me some of Thady Casey's dancing.

The year was 1970 and Breandán Breathnach was working on his book *Folk Music and Dances of Ireland*. Breandán was not a dancer, and as he knew that I was living in Clare at the time, he wrote to me and asked me to provide him with detail on some dance terms. He suggested that I call to see Jimmy Ward, a member of the Kilfenora Céilí Band who lived locally, to see if he could help. Jimmy was happy to oblige and it was thus that I conducted my first interview on dance. In Jimmy's snug kitchen I listened fascinated as a whole world unfolded. He talked of a "fund-raising dance" during the 1930s when the "detectives" – members of the police force based in the area – raided the house and every man was punched and kicked as the dancers were ejected from the premises. Jimmy was spared a beating that time as he was a visiting musician from a different part of Clare. The police action was taken ostensibly on foot of the recently enacted Public Dance Hall Act (1935). The act effectively banned dances in the houses of rural Ireland and put pressure on people to attend only formally organised dances in the newly built halls, most of which were run by the local clergy, and did not find favour with the people who had previously organised their own dances on all kinds of occasions. Jimmy went on to talk of happier events: card playing combined with dancing, "tournaments", "swarees", and "joined dances", when the jollity sometimes went on all night and the company returned to their homes as the sun was rising in the sky. He also gave me the information that Breandán wanted. What did the dance terms puzzle, shuffle and drum mean precisely and what exactly was the rising step of the jig? I sent off the information to Breandán and he pronounced himself satisfied with the results.

Meanwhile, my curiosity about the dance world sketched by Jimmy Ward was aroused and I was determined to find out more. I also was keen to discover if anybody still could do the old-style step dancing which Jimmy had referred to in my interviews with him. He suggested I talk to Martin Talty, a well-known local musician, who was a great friend of Breandán Breathnach. It was Martin who suggested Willie Clancy as a source. Willie's memory was phenomenal and encyclopaedic, and Martin felt that he was my best bet. That is how I came to spend many happy winter's nights at Willie's and his wife Doreen's fireside.

Of course, not all the talk was of dance. Willie was a wonderful raconteur and he had many's the wry and witty comment on the world at large. He was always joking. One day when a friend called looking for the loan of a "single rule", Doreen answered the door and called out to Willie. Willie shouted back, "Ask him will a married one do him!"

I was often hesitant to get him to show me a step as, even though he was only in his fifties, he would get terribly breathless after only a few moments dancing and would have to hold on to a chair for support. As he danced, he lilted the "Harvest Home" hornpipe, and my memory is indelibly imprinted with the accompanying sound of the coins jingling rhythmically in the pockets of the dungarees which were the badge of his craft of carpenter.

A regular visitor to the house was the flute-player of the Kilfenora Céilí Band, J.C. Talty, who had been Willie and Doreen's best man. He was intrigued to see Willie teaching me to dance. He was there one evening when I called. Willie answered the door and I knew by him that he had a story for me.

"I had Doreen awake half the night last night. She hadn't a minute's peace with me," he began.

Doreen blushed and giggled. "Willie, you're an awful man. Don't be saying things like that."

I waited for Willie to continue because I knew the punchline had yet to come. It was true that Doreen had had a sleepless night, but it was all because Willie had lain awake for hours tapping and re-tapping the foot of the bed as he struggled to remember a hornpipe step he had learnt from Thady Casey some thirty years before.

"It's a step for finishing off; a real showstopper."

And indeed it was. Involving a mighty flurry of double batters, its rhythms resounding through the flags of the floor, it sprang to life under the flying feet. Thady was at this stage in his nineties and virtually immobilised by age, but that night the walls echoed to his genius via Willie's dancing. I felt that I had been given a marvellous present – a rare glimpse into the past.

It was the last step Willie ever taught me. Life brought me back to the east coast to a new job, to marriage and settling into an unfamiliar town. I vowed to return to Miltown to get the jig and the reel that Willie had in his memory, but I could not foresee as I left the town in June 1971 that I would never see him again. His untimely death robbed us all of his priceless and deeply individual genius. The next time I saw Clare was to shake Jimmy Ward's hand as we struggled – in my case unsuccessfully – to control our tears on the day of Willie's funeral in January 1972. Friel's pub was packed to the doors that day and the session was mighty. It was so noisy, so different from the calm winter's nights I had spent there in Willie's company beneath the photo of the 1932 Eucharistic Congress ("A Million Kneel at Benediction in O'Connell Street"), with the wag-o'-the wall ticking and Maisie and Tom Friel, their voices gentle and wistful, remembering the myriad singers, dancers and musicians who had crowded their pub over the years. Willie recalled a time when Séamus Ennis, his friend, rival and fellow-piper, was lodging in Friel's. It was noon one day when Séamus appeared on the stairs. Halfway down he stopped to intone in his famously sonorous tones, "I'm *up* but I'm not *down*. I'm *down* but I'm not *up*."

Maisie wheezed with laughter. "I remember, I remember. There's no doubt; he was a holy terror, poor Séamus."

Willie's death was a bitter reminder that time could rob us suddenly of someone who seemed likely to live for many a long year, and I felt I just had to document whatever was left of the old-style dance of the region. Willie had brought me out to see Thady Casey in 1970 and I had picked up the names of three local dancers. One of them was a former pupil of Thady's, John Joe Moroney from near Spanish Point. The two other men, Jimmo Sexton of Mullagh and Jimmy Quin, had been taught by Pat Barron, a Limerickman who operated in the area around Mullagh. In 1976, a friend of mine, Roy Esmonde, had just bought a video camera, which was a newfangled device at that time, and I arranged for him to film the three dancers in Johnny Burke's pub, the Armada in Spanish Point. The musicians were Jimmy Ward and P.J. Murrihy. Jimmo Sexton skipped around the floor like a two year old. He danced a sprightly, puckish reel and a version of a dance which Barron specialised in – "Mount Phoebus' Hunt" – which was amazingly complicated and required a high degree of dancing skill. Later that day, the recording moved to the school in Miltown when John Joe Moroney danced a jig, a dance which was later described to me as "a cross [difficult] dance", and the "Job of Journeywork". "And well able," as he said himself. This time the musicians were the redoubtable Bobby Casey and John Kelly.

INTRODUCTION

It is sobering to look over that old black-and-white footage now and reflect how easily those wonderful dancers could have died without leaving any record behind, as so many did. Since that recording in 1976, I have made many field trips all over Ireland. Doing fieldwork is not always as romantic as it sounds. It can be exhilarating, exhausting, fruitful, frustrating, eventful and tedious by turn. One thing it is not is predictable, and when the talk is flowing freely, the equipment is "motoring" and, best of all, when the dust is flying under the capering feet, the effect is magical.

Some of the best recording sessions happened in people's own homes where their dance memories crowded the rooms. I talked to Harry and Catherine Fairtclough in their house in the shadow of Millmount, in the Duleek Gate area of Drogheda, where Cromwell breached the walls. They had an old version of "Lannigan's Ball", and it was through them that the dance world of Louth began to unfold. Later, I heard stories of the wonderful dancing of Jimmy Markey of Oulster Lane who made dancing dolls for the local children. He also made himself a set of metal false teeth, but that's a different story. Fintan Rafferty, who used to bottle beer in Caitlín Bean Uí Chairbre's dockside pub and who later went to sea and was tragically drowned in a foreign port, told me to go and see his mother Molly if I wanted to know about dancing. Molly and her brother, Jem Darby, told me of dancing sets at the three-crossroads near Beaulieu on sunny summer evenings, with the music echoing over the water to Mornington. Everything I heard seemed to say to me that, contrary to the received wisdom, Irish dance was not something that existed only in remote mountain fastnesses or in certain designated areas of rural Ireland. In fact, it was there in every city, town and village in the country, just waiting to be uncovered.

One marvellously memorable trip was down to Labasheeda, County Clare, in 1989 to meet Dan Furey and James Keane. Dan was in his eighties at the time and was still teaching dancing. When my friend Alison Kelly and I pulled up outside the community hall in the village, Dan was already there with his old Morris Minor full to the brim with sandwiches and dancers. Over the space of two days, we recorded what amounted to the entire dance repertoire of the area – from sets to the valeta waltz, the barndance, the scottische, three- and six-hand reels, the solo jig and hornpipe, the "Gabhairín Buí" (a rare dance over two crossed sticks), "single time" to single jig time and the "Priest in his Boots", which had been mentioned in an old handbook of Irish dance in 1902 and which had been assumed to be extinct, which I had first recorded from Tom Synan of Doonbeg in 1984.

Other field trips, to the four corners of Ireland have unearthed material which is fascinating in its richness and diversity. A "Trip to Sligo" in 1996 brought evidence of a nest of dancers around Gurteen, such as Mick Dyer and Tommy Killoran, whose dancing complements the genius of their friend the flute-player Seamus Tansey, and whose steps are as wild and free as his music. On the far side of the country in County Cavan, a dance known locally as the "Dorricles", which appears to be an old country dance and has never been mentioned in any previous accounts, has recently come to light. The story is still being told. We just have to be there to hear it.

The world of Irish traditional dance is in many ways the equivalent of the oral tradition of singing and storytelling and emanates from the same social class, the so-called "plain people of Ireland". This book is their story. Its voices are primarily theirs. But beneath the words is another sound: the echo of tapping, stamping, drumming feet. They reverberate down the centuries and resound from the floors and walls of deserted cabins, the timbers of emigrant ships, the stages of the cities of America and Britain, the platforms of roadside "dancing decks"; from tables, barrel tops, half-doors; indeed, from any surface which could amplify that most insistent beat of Irish life – the rhythm of the dance.

Behind the book is a quest into the heartland of the dance, that largely uncharted territory which is marked by elements of sociology, culture, politics and religion – a heady mixture, by any account. It is altogether astonishing that the practice of dance, which the indefatigable Captain Francis O'Neill,[1] the renowned music collector who was chief of police in Chicago in the late 1800s – early 1900s, was prompted to defend as "a legitimate amusement", has long been the focus of contention and condemnation from official sources, whether secular or clerical. In these pages, we will relive the controversies, re-evaluate the commentaries and, above all, salute the dancers, both living and dead.

---

1   Capt. Francis O'Neill, Irish Minstrels and Musicians (Cork: Mercier Press, 1987), p. 417. Originally published Chicago, 1913.

Chapter One

The History of Dance in Earlier Times

D ANCE IS, BY its nature, ephemeral. One moment the air resounds to the tapping of feet and the lilt of the accompanying music. Then, the silence surges softly backwards and the swirling energy of the dancers' movements is but a fleeting memory. Our account begins long before any notation of dance was thought possible or, indeed, necessary. Dance nowadays is automatically part of a celebration such as a wedding or a rite of passage event such as a school graduation. Similarly, in earlier times, dancing was considered an integral part of social gatherings; so much so, indeed, that it was not seen as essential or even appropriate to record it in any detail.

The documentary evidence of dance in Ireland begins in the Middle Ages. Apart from one brief, oft-quoted allusion to dance in an early English poem dating from the 1300s, "Ich am of Irlaunde. Come and daunce with me in Irlaunde", (which may simply be an English poet using Ireland as an exotic location in his verse), references to dancing in Ireland in the years prior to the early seventeenth century are few and far between. Even where the Irish words for dance – *rince* and *damhsa* – do occur, it is not possible to glean any information as to the precise nature of the dance. The earliest references to *rince* – "*Rainge timcheall teinne ag buidhin tseibhir treinneartmhuir"* [1] (A dance around fires by a slender swift vigorous group) – dates from 1588. The earliest reference to *damhsa* dates from 1510 and is somewhat enigmatic: *"Cidh na dena damhsa frit cosaibh?"*[2] (Why do you not dance with your feet?)

It is not until the seventeenth century that we have any real documentary accounts referring to dance. This is by no means confined to Ireland. Worldwide, dance scholarship in general is hampered by the lack of contemporary records pre-1600s. It is often the interested visitor whose observations provide us with insights. In the Irish context, agents of the English crown feature prominently. Fynes Moryson, a representative of Elizabeth I, writes in 1600:

> They [the Irish] delight in dansing using no artes of slow measures or lofty Galliards but only countrey dances whereof they have some pleasant to behold as "Balrudery'" and "The Whip of Dunboyne" and they danse about a fyer (commonly in the midst of the room), holding withies in their hands and by certain straynes drawing one another into the fyer and also the matachine dances with naked swords which they make to meet in divers comely postures."[3]

Moryson's reference to "countrey dances" is interesting in that it identifies the presence in Ireland of dances apparently similar to the English "country dances" of the period. At this time in England the popular dances of the village had become the social dances of polite society. According to Joan Flett, an expert in English and Scottish social dance, "It is probable that the country dances would have lost a great deal of their simplicity and some of their vigour in the transition from a rural to a more sophisticated situation. They would have been affected by the dress and manners of the times, would have been polished and may well have been influenced by dances introduced from abroad."[4]

---

1   James D. Carney, ed., *Poems on the Butlers of Ormond, Cahir and Dunboyne* (Dublin: Dublin Institute for Advanced Studies, 1945), p. 79.
2   Referred to in Breandán Breathnach, *Dancing in Ireland* (Miltown Malbay, Co. Clare: Dal gCais Publications, 1983), p. 14.
3   C. Litton Falkiner, *Illustrations of Irish History and Topography,* (London: New York and Boston, 1904), p. 322.
4   Joan Flett, *Social Dancing in England from the 17th Century,* Vaughan Williams Memorial Library Leaflet No. 18, n.d., p. 3.

The earliest documentation of country dances reveals a group dance with many different formations. A man and a woman danced together as partners; with other couples; in a circle, square, a single line or in a double line with the men in one line and the women in another.

Moryson, as an agent of the crown, would have been present at the Elizabethan court where, we are told: "We are frolic here at court; much dancing in the privy chamber of country dances before the queen's majesty; who is exceeding pleased therewith. Irish tunes are at this time much liked."[5]

It is a matter for speculation whether the country dances referred to by Moryson had an identifiably Irish form, but it seems highly likely that group dance was part of the native Irish tradition in this period.

Moryson's account is also the earliest reference to the Irish sword and withy dances. The popularity of these dances in seventeenth century Ireland is attested by other writers. Two extracts from seventeenth century Irish poets are given here. The first, dating from 1669, details the prevalent social customs in an Irish chieftain's house:

Rinnce an ghadairigh ag aicme den chóip sin
Rinnce an chlaidhimh do dhlighe gach ordeir,
Rinnce treasach le malartaibh ceolta
Is rinnce fada le racaireacht ógbhan.[6]

(The withy dance by some of the company
The sword dance which commands order
The dance in ranks with change of tempo
And the long dance with the sporting of maidens.)

These lines are extremely interesting in that they document not alone the sword and withy dances but also make reference to a dance in ranks – a country dance? – and a long-line dance which seems to indicate a "Carole" or serpentine dance formation among the native Irish in the seventeenth century.

---

5   Extract from a letter from the Earl of Worcester to the Earl of Shrewsbury, quoted in John Nichol, *The Progresses and Public Processions of Queen Elizabeth*, vol. 3 (London: John Nichols and Son, 1823), p. 40.

6   In a *Caoineadh* by Domhnall Garbh Ó Súilleabháin, Ms. 23 N 12, 157, Royal Irish Academy.

Another seventeenth century poem mentions *"rince an chlaidhimh is rince an ghadaraidh"*[7] as being danced through the gates of the town on the accession of the Catholic James II to the throne of England. The implication here is that these dances would normally have been done outside the town boundaries in the haunts of the native "rebel" Irish and represent a genuine account of Irish dance practice in this period.

The main source of information on the dance customs of the Irish in the late seventeenth century is provided by a number of English visitors. Their accounts confirm that dancing was universal on Sundays and holidays. The music was provided by a piper or fiddler with occasional performance by a harper or "Jews harp" player. The Irish passion for dance is well expressed by one Richard Head who, writing in 1620, tells us: "Their Sunday is the most leisure day they have in which they use all manner of sport; in every field a fiddle and the lasses footing it till they are all of a foam."[8]

As to the form of the dance, we meet further references to the long dance or *rince fada* in an account by Thomas Dineley written in 1681: "They are at this day much addicted (on holidayes after the bagpipe, Irish Harpe or Jewes Harpe) to danse after their countrey fashions [that is] the long dance one after another of all conditions, Master, Mrs., servants."[9]

This description is interesting in that it suggests that dance occasions offered the opportunity for all classes to mingle, whereas otherwise they might be obliged to maintain a discreet distance.

Another seventeenth century visitor, John Dunton, makes it clear that he regarded the Irish as being generally uncouth. He cannot refrain from displaying his prejudice as he describes various Irish social customs. Of an Irish wedding, he says: "After the matrimonial ceremony was over we had a Bag Piper and a blind harper that *dinn'd us* [my italics] with their music to which there was perpetuall dancing."[10] Another of his references

---

7   Rev. J.C. McErlean, *Duanaire Dháibhidh Uí Bhruadair*, part iii, (London: 1916–7), pp. 110–11.
8   Richard Head, *The Western Wonder* (1670), p. 37.
9   Thomas Dineley, *Voyage through the Kingdom of Ireland in the Year* 1841 (Dublin: M.H. Gill, 1870), p. 19.
10   Extract from John Dunton's letters, printed as an appendix in Edward Mc Lysaght, *Irish Life in the Seventeenth Century After Cromwell*. (Dublin and Cork, 1939, 1950), p. 359.

tells us that, at a wake: "Sometimes they followed one another in a ring (as they say fairies do) in a rude dance to the music of a bagpipe."[11].

Another important social event at which dancing played a major part was the "pattern" or celebration of a local patron saint's day. Whilst the event was primarily of a religious nature, it was common for the day to end in secular amusements. Some details of the customs associated with a pattern are given by Sir Henry Piers in 1682:

> On the patron-day in most parishes, as also on the feasts of Easter and Whitsuntide, the more ordinary sort of people meet near the ale-house in the afternoon, on some convenient spot of ground and dance for the cake; here to be sure the piper fails not of diligent attendance; the cake to be danced for is provided at the charge of the ale wife, and is advanced on a board on the top of a pike about ten foot high; this board is round and from it riseth a kind of a garland, beset and tied round with meadow flowers, if it be early in the summer, if later, the garland has the addition of apples set round on pegs fastened unto it; the whole number of dancers begin all at once in a large ring, a man and a woman, and dance round about the bush, so is this garland called and the piper, as long as they are able to hold on; they that hold out longest at the exercise, win the cake and apples, and then the ale-wife's trade goes on.[12]

On ceremonial occasions such as the arrival of an honoured guest or, it seems, on May Eve, the *rince fada* was paramount. An observer detailing the arrival from England of James II at Kinsale in March 1689 and his progress to Dublin tells us that "all along the road the country came to meet his majesty . . . the young rural maids weaving dances before him as he travelled . . ."[13]

A much more comprehensive description of the dance which greeted the king is given in an account dated 1780. We are tempted to doubt the accuracy of such belated testimony. However the details are interesting and are thus quoted in full:

---

11   *Ibid*, p. 350.

12   Sir Henry Piers, A *Chorographical History of the County Westmeath*, quoted in Kevin Dana-her, *The Year in Ireland* (Cork: The Mercier Press, 1972), p. 80.

13   J.T. Gilbert, ed., A *Jacobite Narrative of the War in Ireland, 1688–1691* (Shannon, Co. Clare: Irish University Press, 1971), p. 46.

Three persons abreast each holding the ends of a white hand-kerchief first moved forward a few paces to slow music; the rest of the dancers followed 2 by 2, a white hand-kerchief between each. Then the dance began. The music suddenly changing to brisk time, the dancers passed with a quick step under the hand-kerchief of the three in front, wheeled around in semi-circles, formed a variety of pleasing animating evolutions interspersed with entire chants or cuts united and fell again into their original places and paused.[14]

This picturesque description of the *rince fada* with the unusual feature of the use of handkerchiefs indicates a further evolution of the dance in the seventeenth century.

The Irish passion for dancing continued into the eighteenth century. Writing in 1775, an English visitor called Rev. Dr Campbell tells us:

The Irish girls are passionately fond of dancing, and they certainly dance well, for last night I was at a ball and I never enjoyed one more in my life. There is a sweet affability and sparkling vivacity in these girls which is very captivating. We frog-blooded English dance as if the practice were not congenial to us; but here [in Cashel] they moved as if dancing had been the business of their lives.[15]

The keenly observant traveller Arthur Young in his *Tour of Ireland* (1776–1779) noted: "Dancing is very general among the poor people. Almost universal in every cabbin . . . Weddings are always celebrated with much dancing." Referring to the dances, he says: "Besides the Irish jig which they can dance with a most luxuriant expression, minuets and country dances are taught and I even heard some talk of cotillons coming in."[16]

Young is obviously very well aware of dance fashion. He is evidently struck by the fact that the cotillon, which had relatively recently achieved popularity in the upper class salons of English society, should have penetrated so quickly into the heart of Irish rural society. We, in turn, are not surprised by Young's reference to country dances since their popularity in

---

14 Joseph C. Walker, *Historical Memories of the Irish Bards*, 2nd ed. (Dublin, 1818), p. 1215.
15 Quoted in Capt. Francis O'Neill, *Irish Minstrels and Musicians* (Cork: Mercier Press, 1987), p. 417. Originally published Chicago, 1913.
16 Arthur Young, *A Tour in Ireland* (London: Bell, 1892), p. 1446.

Irish circles had been well attested to by various commentators since 1600 at least. Similarly, the jig already had a long association with Ireland.

Given its present dominance in music and dance, it may seem surprising that the reel is a relative latecomer to the Irish scene. Scholars are agreed that the reel as a dance tempo with its associated faster figures and stepping did not attain universal popularity in Ireland until the late eighteenth century – early nineteenth century, whereas across the water in Scotland it had long existed in twosome, threesome, foursome, sixsome and eightsome forms. Despite its late arrival in Ireland, the reel was to become central in the world of Irish music and dance from the late eighteenth century onwards. The old sixteenth century dance known as the hay (hey, haye), which appears to be of French origin, involved a movement where the dancers performed a figure-of-eight or reeling pattern. An interesting survival of what seems to be the early figure-of-eight or reeling figure associated with the hay comes to us from Wexford. Patrick Kennedy describes a dance from around 1815 locally known as the "reel-of-three" in which "at points in the dance the three were engaged in performing evolutions which they were pleased to call the figure-of-eight". The tempo was described as being "in the style of a jig but to slower time, one performer standing inactive in the rear and displacing the one immediately before him at the proper time".[17]

A sole reference in 1718 to the hornpipe is contained in a dancing master's contract between William Bailey, gentleman, and Charles Staunton, dancing master, in which the employer directs that his children be taught "jigs, minuets, hornpipe and country dance".[18] The hornpipe referred to here is not necessarily a solo dance, as the hornpipe measure was also used in some country dances. Playford's *The English Dancing Master*, first published in 1651,[19] contained some country dance hornpipes, the music being printed with dance instructions. This manual may have been used by the above Charles Staunton. Whatever the case, even a cursory glance at the hornpipe tunes contained therein shows that they differ radically

17   Patrick Kennedy, "Irish Dancing Fifty Years Ago", *Dublin University Magazine*, vol. LXII (1863), p. 435.
18   JRSAI, vol. 18 (1887–8), p. 213.
19   John Playford, *The English Dancing Master* (London: 1651).

in character from what is now recognised as an Irish hornpipe measure. The typical accented rhythm of the hornpipe as it is danced in Ireland nowadays was not developed until the 1760s.

It has been suggested that the hornpipe dance as we know it was imported here from the English stage towards the end of the eighteenth century. At this period, the stage hornpipe was of the "sailors' hornpipe" variety which falls into the category of a high dance, danced to light hopping and skipping movements akin to Scottish stepping, as distinct from a "step dance" which is characterised by the beating out with the feet of the musical rhythms accompanying the dancer and which formed part of the living English and Scottish heritage. Indeed, in many areas of Britain such as Lancashire, Cumbria, Norfolk, Suffolk, Devon and the Western Isles and east coast of Scotland, we find evidence of "stepping" which contains elements similar to and in some cases identical to the Irish steps. The close connections between, for example, Ireland and Lancashire in the form of Irish migrant labour in the cotton mills would point to the likelihood of an input by these workers into the dance of their temporary home abroad as well as the possibility that they carried steps home with them.

The most influential agents in the spread of dance innovations in the late eighteenth century were the dancing masters such as Charles Staunton. In common with their counterparts in western Europe generally, they were instrumental in developing individual dance skills in terms of stepping as well as teaching the currently fashionable group dances, such as the country dance. By now, this term meant longways dances, and Irish forms were published in great numbers in eighteenth and nineteenth century Dublin.

Travellers in Ireland in the early 1800s attest to the continued popularity of dancing amongst the people. John Carr, who toured the country in 1805, says:

A Sunday with the peasantry in Ireland was not unlike the same day in France. After the hours of devotion a spirit of gaiety shines upon every hour, the bagpipe is heard, and every foot is in motion. The cabin on this day is deserted, and families in order to meet together and enjoy the luxury of a social chat, even in rain and snow, will walk three or four miles to a given spot.[20]

On a Sunday in 1812, an English visitor, John Gamble, accompanied by a horrified "strict Sabbatarian" friend, was amazed by the scene he came upon outside Dundalk. "The fields were swarming with people, men, women and children, running, wrestling, throwing long bullets and dancing. This latter was fully as violent an exercise as any of the others and consisted in a continued and violent agitation of the limbs and body.[21]

Whereas the main event of the eighteenth century in dance terms had been the introduction of the reel and hornpipe measures, the nineteenth century saw the arrival here of the quadrille, a dance which was to sweep the country and which has survived in modified form to the present day. The quadrilles were based on a modification of the old English square-eight formation which had died out in the seventeenth century. In the eighteenth century, this square-eight dance had a rebirth in the form of the French contradanse and cotillon (from the French for petticoat). The cotillon had already achieved some popularity here in Ireland. As we have said, Arthur Young, the eighteenth century traveller heard of it "coming in" and another account tells us that in Wexford in 1813 at a crossroads dance: "by general acclamation 'peticoatees' and 'coatylongs' [cotillons] were introduced and postured through to the air of the Jackson family".[22] The reference here to the dance being "postured through" suggests a perception by the author of the difference in style and performance between this type of imported ballroom dance and the livelier native forms.

The quadrille is an early nineteenth century adaptation of these earlier square-eight dances in which four couples take part, each couple standing on a side of a small square facing into the centre of the square.

The first performance of the "First Set of Quadrilles" quadrille in Ireland took place in 1816 in Dublin. This selection or "suite" – later, "set" – of dances comprised:

---

20   John Carr, *The Stranger in Ireland* (Shannon, Co. Clare: Irish University Press, 1970), pp. 255-6. Originally published 1806.
21   John Gamble, *A View of Society and Manners in the North of Ireland* (London: 1813), p. 25.
22   Patrick Kennedy, "Irish Dancing Fifty Years Ago", p. 439.

1. – Le pantalon (in 6/8 time);
2. – L'été (in 6/8 time);
3. – La poule (in 2/4 time);
4. – La pastourelle (in 2/4 time);
5. – La finale (in 6/8 time).

Within months the resultant quadrille craze would produce a whole raft of newly composed dances to meet the intense public demand. As with the "First Set", these were based on the older contradanse and cotillon figures. Amongst them are the lancers, which was first advertised in the *Dublin Evening Post* on 1 May 1817, the Alberts, the Caledonians, and the Parisian Quadrille.

In a County Louth newspaper[23], in 1844, we find the following advertisement:

Just Published
THE DUBLIN AND DISTRICT RAILWAY QUADRILLES.
Dedicated to Sir John MacNeil, L.L.D.[24]
Price Three Shillings.
To be had at P. Kent's Music Shop, West-street, Drogheda, and at the
Publishers, Marcus Moses, 4, Westmoreland-street, Dublin.
The above admired Quadrilles will be forwarded to any part of the
Kingdom, postage free, on receipt of a Post-office Order for 3s. 6d.

The advertisement goes on to say that: "Messrs. Kent's Quadrille Band will attend any distance in the country as usual."

A commentator on the ballroom style of dancing quadrilles in the nineteenth century writes:

For many years it has now been the custom in the higher grades of society to simply walk through the figures of quadrilles. It is doubtless owing to the elimination of all steps of a lively nature that the practice of square dances has come to be regarded as an intolerable bore by the frequenters of fashionable ballrooms and indeed when we come to consider the fact that most of

---

23 *Drogheda Argus*, 15 June 1844.
24 The Sir John MacNeil to whom the quadrilles are dedicated was the engineer who designed the viaduct over the river Boyne at Drogheda on the Great Northern Railway between Belfast and Dublin.

the modern votaries of Terpsicore, if such they may fairly be called, especially the males, are entirely innocent of any true conception of gracefulness, it is not a matter of wonder that they find little pleasure in going through what must appear to them uncommonly like unsystematic drill evolutions.[25]

This description with its picture of unenthusiastic dancers and the absence of any steps of a lively nature is in marked contrast to an account by P.W. Joyce of an Irish eight-hand reel where the dancers

. . . first stand in a circle around the room and then go through a regular series of complicated evolutions somewhat like the figures of a quadrille but much more animated as all are continually in motion. In these movements there are regularly recurring pauses during which the women stand still, while the men exercise themselves to their hearts content in "thribbling" taking particular care, during these intervals, however short, never to allow a single bar or note of the music to go waste.[26]

Another writer tells us:

Let not the frequenters of more refined reunions wonder if we suspect that the enjoyment of a reel by its four performers face-to-face and sympathising with each other exceeds very considerably that of my Lord Dundreary and his partner listlessly walking a quadrille."[27]

The quadrille sets (or half-sets for two couples), as they came to be known among the people, were obviously first and foremost ballroom dances but, as often happens, the popularity of a dance measure knows no social barriers, and these dances moved gradually from the ballrooms of "polite" society (generally via the dancing masters or local dance enthusiasts) to the country houses and crossroads of rural Ireland, as well as to urban centres. However, far from simply adopting these new dances wholesale, the Irish dance tradition absorbed the sets and made of them something new in terms of figures, musical tempo and stepping.

The transformation wrought on the quadrilles in Ireland was produced by a combination of factors: the adoption of jig, reel and hornpipe

---

25 Edward Scott, *Dancing: As an Art and Pastime* (London: G. Bell, 1892), pp. 136–7.
26 George Petrie, *Ancient Music of Ireland* (Dublin: 1855), p. 60.
27 Patrick Kennedy, "Irish Dancing Fifty Years Ago", p. 435.

measures which had the effect of increasing the tempo of the dance; the application of the Irish "travelling steps" and the subtly ornamental features of the solo jig and reel steps in place of the "marching step" of the quadrilles; and finally the cross-fertilisation of the new imports with elements of the older jig and reel group dances, resulting in a new and identifiably Irish product.

Oral tradition and the folk memory tell us exactly how and when the sets were introduced into different areas in rural Ireland. Big Mike Newman, who used to frequent the ordinary kitchen dances in the neighbouring parish of Carrick Edmond, introduced the sets in Ballinalee, County Longford. This happened about 1870. Around 1880 a man called Callaghan, a renowned dancer from Flagmount, introduced the sets to Tulla in County Clare. Florrie Brosnahan, a dancing master from north Kerry, we are told, brought them to Uíbh Ráthach in South Kerry around 1890. Dan Furey, the dancing master from Labasheeda, County Clare, remarks that the Caledonian set came into his area around the 1930s, "but did not take over the other sets", whereas "the old crowd used to dance the 'Orange and Green' and the 'Lancers'".[28] It is recorded that the sets reached County Cavan in the 1870s or 1880s.

Again, acceptance of these new dances was by no means universal. Éibhlín Ní Mhurchú, in an account of the music and dance of the Corca Dhuibhne area of Kerry (where the sets were introduced by Florie McCarthy from Oileán Chiarraí after 1880), says: "*Bhí seanbhlas ag na seandaoine ar na seiteanna.*" "The old people had contempt for the sets." She quotes one such elderly critic, whose uncompromising judgement, "*Níl ann ach tónachas anois,*" can be rendered as, "There's nothing in them but arsing about." Another member of the older generation saw the sets as involving "ignorant people throwing their feet every which way" ("*daoine díchéillí ag caitheamh a gcos trína chéile*").[29] Despite such opposition, the sets took root and flourished, and by the end of the nineteenth century they had penetrated every county in Ireland.

---

28   Larry Lynch, *Set Dances of Ireland: Tradition and Evolution* (Miltown Malbay, Co. Clare: Séadna Books, in collaboration with Dal gCais Publications, 1989), p. 93.

29   Eibhlín Ní Mhurchú, *Ceol agus Rinnce Mo Cheantair Dúchais ó 1800–1880* (Baile an Fheirtéaraigh, Co. Chiarraí: Oidhreacht Chorca Dhuibhne, 1990), p. 120.

Certain areas became associated with particular sets. In Clare, for example, the Caledonian set was exceptionally popular, whereas Kerry and Cork became the home of a proliferation of sets including the Jenny Lind (Ginny Ling), the Victoria and the Talavara or Televara. The Set of Erin and the Orange and Green were danced in the south and south-west of the country and seem, from their names, to have been specially created for the Irish market. Certain sets adopted the name of the locality in which they were danced, such as the Cashel and Ballycommon sets of County Tipperary.

Occasionally, the usual pattern of five or six "figures" with a break between each figure was not followed. For instance, in Counties Monaghan[30] and Fermanagh[31], the set consisted of one long unbroken sequence danced to jig time. The sets on the Aran Islands of County Galway also consisted of one long unbroken sequence. These regional variations would seem to be a fascinating example of the extent to which the original structure of the "set of quadrilles" was altered in some regions of Ireland. An alternative explanation of such entirely untypical sets as these in Counties Fermanagh and Monaghan and in Aran is that they are possibly survivors of an older pre-set dance which, under the influence of the quadrille craze, simply underwent a change of name whilst maintaining intact their original structure.

Amongst the most universally popular of the sets were the lancers and the mazurka. The mazurka emerged as the mazolka in Monaghan, the mazorka in Donegal, the myserks in Clare and the mesarts in Kerry. Originally the mazurka set had its own music but eventually it came to be danced to reels. The set of lancers was danced from Antrim to Wexford and from Mayo to Meath. The sets were, of course, equally popular in Britain, and I was amused to hear from two prominent Gaelic League members from Drogheda – Harry Fairtclough and his wife Catherine – that

---

30 Owen Smyth (national teacher), Knockconan, near Emyvale, Co. Monaghan, tells us that the set in that area was "unlike the Kerry set – no change of tempo and much shorter – 4 couples to each set – jig time." Irish Folklore Commission dance questionnaire (1969).

31 The set as danced in the area around Beleek in Fermanagh was recorded on video by Seán Corcoran in 1985, and it scotches the notion that all sets in Ireland followed the pattern of a series of figures with a break between each one.

they loved going to dances in Butlin's Holiday Camp in Mosney, County Meath, in the 1930s because the Scots visitors were "great at the sets and it was a pleasure to dance with them".

Apart from the sets, the most popular new dances in the nineteenth century were the ballroom dances such as the scottische, the barndance, the military two-step and the waltz, which became part of the dance practice of all classes of society. When they reached the areas where traditional dance was strong, they were absorbed into the repertoire and subtly changed by the effects of Irish "stepping" and local musical tastes.

Without doubt, the nineteenth century had seen an enormous change in the repertoire of traditional dancers in Ireland. Once again, the living tradition had absorbed new forms and made of them something distinctively Irish. However, as the century turned, the whole notion of what was and what was not acceptable to Irish dancing feet became an issue for those who would seek to "preserve" the tradition in some idealised form. The world of dance was about to come under scrutiny as never before.

Chapter Two

The Fleshpots of Egypt and Gaelic Mayo: Dance and the Gaelic League

C ENTRAL TO THE events which shaped the world of Irish dance at the turn of the twentieth century was the foundation, in 1893, of *Conradh na Gaeilge* (the Gaelic League). The League's main interest was in the promotion of the Irish language, and initially its involvement in the area of dance was peripheral. Somewhat surprisingly, the impetus came from London where the League had a flourishing branch. One of the most energetic and charismatic of the League's organisers, Fionán Mac Coluim,[1] was working as a clerk in the India Office in the late 1890s. Also prominent in the organisation in London was J.G. O'Keeffe, who worked in the war office. Whilst their Irish language classes were operating successfully, they were keenly aware of the lack of a social dimension to their activities, particularly when they attended some lively Scots *céilithe* in London.

---

[1] Fionán Mac Coluim (1875–1966) was born in County Antrim but spent much of his childhood in the Kerry *Gaeltacht*. He worked tirelessly for the Irish language movement, and many feel that he did not get the recognition he deserved during his lifetime. Though he obviously spent a considerable amount of time drafting and redrafting material relating to dance, he unfortunately did not publish anything of note on the topic.

Mac Coluim and others decided to take positive action, and the first ever Irish *céilí* – a Gaelic word meaning "an evening visit, a friendly call" was held in the Bloomsbury Hall near the British Museum on Saturday, 30 October 1897. Amongst the invited guests were a group of Scottish dancers and singers and some Welsh singers, who performed on stage. The dance programme proved a problem. The majority of the Gaelic League members in London were white-collar workers – journalists, doctors and civil servants – and, according to Mac Coluim's account, their knowledge of Irish dance was limited.[2]

Most, however, knew the basic form of the double jig danced in couples with a row of men facing a row of women: all move around the room for 8 bars, then dance for 8 bars opposite partner, change places, dance new step, change back to place, and so on. The only other dances known to the company were the quadrilles and the waltz, which were performed by "Fitzgerald's Band" to Irish airs in honour of the occasion.

The contrast between this *céilí* and the contemporaneous Scottish events with their profusion of dances was not lost on Mac Coluim. He fretted over the problem until fate intervened in the form of an introduction to "Professor" Patrick D. Reidy, then resident in Hackney, originally from Castleisland, County Kerry, who had been a dancing master in west Limerick and Kerry in the late 1800s. Reidy's first classes for Gaelic League members were held in the Bijou Theatre, off the Strand. Here he taught group dances such as the eight-hand reel, the High Caul Cap and a "long dance", sometimes termed by Reidy, "the Kerry reel". Reidy maintained that this was the dance referred to in the eighteenth century folk poem "Cill Chais" (ll. 35-6) which read:

> *go mbeidh rincí fada ag gabháil timpeall,*
> *ceol bheidhlín is tinte cnámh; . . .*
> (dances we'll have in long circles, . . .
> and bone-fires and violin music;)

The excitement generated by the discovery of these dances led to a desire to further explore the field, and a collecting trip to Ireland was soon

2   Fionán Mac Coluim, ms. in the Department of Irish Folklore, University College, Dublin.

organised. The exploratory group included Art O'Brien, later co-author of the League's A *Handbook of Irish Dances*,[3] and Miss Drury, who later under her married name, Mrs Costello was to collect and publish an important collection of Irish-language songs from east Galway, *Amhráin Mhuighe Seóla*.

In 1901, a team of dancers from London attended the *Oireachtas* (the annual gathering of the League) in the Mansion House in Dublin. They demonstrated the four-hand and eight-hand reels to the attendance, with the assistance of the Keating (Dublin) Branch of the League. The enthusiasm of the London Gaelic League for their newly learned dances was contagious. Soon, in conjunction with Irish language classes, the new "*céilí* dances" were being taught by the League's organisers. Classes were also held in traditional step dance. Tim O'Leary from Coal Quay in Cork city was one of the Keating Branch's first teachers. Amongst his pupils were Séamus Ennis's father, Jimmy Ennis, and Jim Brennan (later Séumas Ó Braonáin), my own grandfather. Such was the Keating Branch's interest in dance that it became known as "the Dancing Branch": *agus ní mar mholadh é i gcónaí*[4] ("and this was not necessarily a term of praise"). The tensions implicit in any national cultural organisation during a period of major change began to come to the surface, and it became obvious that the favourable reception of the Keating Branch to the London Gaels' programme of group or figure dances was not necessarily shared by the general membership of the Gaelic League.

During the early 1900s the great debate as to which dances were acceptable and which were not raged in the columns and letter pages of *An Claidheamh Soluis*, the Gaelic League's newspaper, as well as in other publications of the period. The weapons of political debate – vilification, ridicule, scorn and caricature – with their attendant power to wound and alienate, were all employed in the debate which surrounded the attempt to create a canon of Irish dance. The white-hot emotions which informed much of the contributions may seem, at this remove, somewhat overstated and comical, but they provide a fascinating insight into what was, in essence, a cultural civil war with dance as the arena of combat.

---

3   J. G. O'Keefe and Art O'Brien, A *Handbook of Irish Dances* (Dublin: O'Donoghue & Co., 1902).
4   Seumas Ó Braonáin, "Im' Óige", *The Leader*, March 1963.

The fact that much of the League's involvement in dance was initiated in London and in the garrison city of Limerick was used as a weapon by various commentators. The pseudonymous *"Gaedeal"*, writing in the Mayo newspaper, the *Western People*, on 27 August 1904, is particularly vituperative in his criticism of the four- and eight-hand reels (usually termed "figure dances"), which are singled out for attack. He writes:

> Those figure dances were brought to Dublin from London and the city of Limerick and foisted on the Gaelic League as genuinely Irish by some enterprising individuals who saw with their keen Anglicised commercial vision their opportunity of making money. Unfortunately, the Coiste Gnótha [Executive Committee] themselves in 1902 came under the spell of those vulgar, characterless romps, and gave them the hall-mark of the Gaelic League by placing them on the Oireachtas syllabus. From that day to this there has been nothing but wrangling and confusion about the dances in the Gaelic League.

In a further article on 4 September 1904, he maintains: "The apostles of the figure dances urge them as substitutes and antidotes for the round and square dances. But in this way they are perfectly wrong. Their figure dances are jumbles of the quadrilles, the polka, the lancers – the very ones they say they want to avoid."

Gaedeal was not alone in his opinion. In another article, specially commissioned for the *Western People*, the writer opens his case thus: "The remarks made here are written with the best intention, and written solely to point out the shoals and sand-banks, and to show the masters that no detail should be disregarded and no deviation from the true traditional style of dancing should be tolerated."

He attacks the figure dances which are seen as merely an imitation of the quadrilles: "They are the introduction of the 'shoneen'. They and other importations are the 'breath of his nostril'. And why not? the poor 'shoneen' wants to imitate 'Lord 'Arry and Lady 'Arriet'".[5]

The quadrilles, which were by this time spreading through the countryside and becoming "Irishised" in the process, were now banned at Gaelic

---

5   Séumas Ó Braonáin, *"Im' Óige"*, *The Leader*, March 1963.

League *céilithe* (plural of *céilí*). Also excluded as foreign dance were social dances such as the Highland scottische and the barndance, which were at the time part of the repertoire of the ordinary people of rural Ireland, amongst whom traditional dance was strongest.

The decision of the *Coiste Gnótha* to place the contentious four- and eight-hand reels on the syllabus of the 1902 *Oireachtas* – the annual focus of dancing competitions – was the spark which lit the fire. Such was the potential for the dreaded split in the movement occasioned by the controversy over "native" and "alien" dance that it was decided to set up a "Commission of Enquiry" which would sit in public during the *Oireachtas* of 1903. The commission's business was conducted with a great deal of formality. It heard "evidence". It "examined a number of witnesses from the four provinces" and it submitted its report which condemned the "figure dances" as not being Irish.[6] The report was adopted by the *Oireachtas* committee and the *Coiste Gnótha* and the offending four- and eight-hand reels were excluded from the 1904 *Oireachtas* syllabus.

It seems that the ban was not entirely successful, for we are told in a letter from "*Seaghan*" in the *Western People* on 13 June 1904 that: "A couple of figure-dances, like unhappy afterthoughts, got in at the Mayo *Feis* competitions. How did it happen? They were not on the syllabus and they are not Irish."

He concludes his letter with the immortal words:"Is it possible that in Gaelic Mayo there are some who still hanker after the fleshpots of Egypt?"

Despite the best attempts of the leadership of the League, the matter was obviously by no means settled. When the Keating Branch appealed successfully to have the four- and eight-hand reels restored to the 1905 syllabus, on the grounds "that they are so popular" and easy to perform, all hell broke loose.

An editorial comment in the 4 September 1904 edition of *An Claidheamh Soluis* appealed for calm: "We are aware that a great difference of opinion exists on this point, and we think, that, as the matter has now been formally opened, the supporters of each view should see that all the available evidence, documentary and traditional on either side, be produced."

---

6   The findings of the 1903 Gaelic League Commission are reported by *Gaedeal* in the *Western People*, 27 August 1904.

The indomitable *Gaedeal* was unmoved. In a piece which ironically appeared in the *Western People* on the very day of the appeal for reasoned debate, he continues thus:

Those dances are not even caricatures; they are simply brazen impostures and a disgrace to the Gaelic League . . .

. . . There are two classes in the Gaelic League specially interested in running those dances – those having hand-books on dancing to sell and the city quack dancing-masters. The hand-books written by men living in London (one at least of whom has an alarming cockney accent) are ostensibly on Irish dances, but in reality on figure dances, essentially non-Irish. Just fancy learning Irish dancing from books, and worse still, from books inspired in London! Faugh! the thing is impossible . . .

. . . Any clown, no matter how flat-footed or door-footed, leather-heeled, or knock-kneed he may be, can easily and quickly learn these dances, with the result that a number of those pretentious frauds calling themselves professors of traditional Irish dancing have sprung up like mushrooms under the protection of the Gaelic League. Those sordid fellows are making plenty of money by their dances, and obviously it is to their interest to proclaim that they are genuinely Irish.

Irish dances are, like our language, difficult to learn, and the figure dances are so easily learned that the young, thoughtless members are madly rushing to learn them, to the neglect of our own . . . If this state of things continues, we may soon bid good-bye to our Irish dances; they shall soon be as extinct as the dodo.

In a final comment, which gives some indication of the divisive nature of the debate, he concludes:

Now, I think it is evident to anyone who has given the matter a thought that those figure dances are a great danger to the movement by acting as de-Gaelicising and Anglicising agents in the Gaelic League. Had the *Coiste Gnótha* moral fibre enough to put its foot down on the first appearance of those dances, as they were advised by their friends, the round dances and square dances would not be fostered by the Gaelic League in England and Scotland, as I understand they are, and there never would have been those frictions between Gaelic Leaguers about our dances and all would now be working together on true Irish lines.

The controversy rumbled on for a further two years until Éinrí Ó Muireaghasa, one of the most respected members of the League, felt obliged to intervene. In a letter to *An Claidheamh Soluis* on 24 February 1906, he asks:

I will go back to fundamental principles and ask why bother about Irish dancing at all? We find English dances spread all over the country, danced by all classes, popular and easy. Why then disturb this condition of things? What justification is there for upsetting all this and introducing what are in most places new dances? For Irish-Irelanders the all-sufficient justification is that one is distinctively Irish and the other distinctively foreign. It matters not that Irish dances were originally of foreign origin: they have now centuries of occupation in Ireland: they have been assimilated and moulded into their present form by Irish minds and Irish natures, and they are now as typical of Ireland as the erstwhile Roman but now proscribed Irish alphabet – aye – even more so . . .

. . . [W]e all know that it is not on account of any merit or perfection they possess that we have the foreign dances. It is simply because we were half slaves and these were the things danced by our masters. They percolated regularly through the numerous strata of our society from the "court" circles of the Dublin Castle or the Viceregal Lodge, down to that of an "American wake" in a Connacht Hovel.

Ó Muireaghasa proposes a code of practice in relation to dances: older people should not be forced to learn a whole new programme of dances and should be allowed to continue to dance the socially popular dances whether foreign or not. Similarly, women should not be required to make a stand on the notion of whether or not to refuse an invitation to dance a non-Irish dance. This would, he feels, be a problem, from a social point of view.

However, he feels that young men should make a point of dancing Irish dances whenever possible and should politely refuse to take part in "foreign" dances. "It may be a sacrifice, it may be inconvenient, but principle requires it."

Ó Muireaghasa's letter produced an amount of correspondence in *An Claidheamh Soluis*. On 10 March, one Eoghan Brioscó writes:

Is a Frenchman the less French because he dances a waltz, a pas de quatre or an Irish jig? No, certainly not. Then an Irishman is not the less Irish because he waltzes or joins in a set of lancers . . . As regards the statement that Irish dances are superior in grace, science, modesty, life and mental effects, for my part I do not believe it. There is not much science about the see-saw movement in the Irish reel or the jumping about in the jig.

In the same edition, another correspondent maintains:

We ought not to reject a good thing because it is foreign. Without mentioning any of the treasures of art and literature given to the world by Greece and Italy, let us think for a moment of the printing press, the steam engine, and the electric telegraph. Let us be equally indulgent of the quadrille and the waltz, provided always that they are kept in their proper places and in due proportion.

He feels that "in many localities the boycotting of foreign dances would at the present time put an end to all dancing, and even where Irish dances are still in vogue, they are rarely in sufficient variety to fill an evening's entertainment with them alone. We cannot afford to be very drastic in our reform lest we kill the movement by starvation."

In conclusion, he advances the opinion that, "as the jig is the very soul of merriment so is the waltz the poetry of motion".

Again, prompted by this exchange of views, we read in the 24 March 1906 edition of the League's paper a letter condemning the teaching of certain "foreign" dances in convent schools in the west of Ireland. He singles out "baneful suggestive foreign dances such as the polka, the waltz, the Welsh Dance, the Cat Walk, the Cake Walk and all foreign monstrosities" and says that "if there must be innovations, the quadrille or the six or eight-hand reels are not so very bad".

Ó Muireaghasa replies to his critics in the 31 March edition of *An Claidheamh Soluis*. He rejects the suggestion that "foreign" (in other words, English) dances are acceptable and, in a comment which betrays his perception of the likelihood of continuing social and class divisions in the new dawn envisaged by his fellow-Irish Irelanders, he states: "English dancing may be carried on by decent, sober, self-respecting people without perhaps any harm but among rough ignorant folk, and with country youths bubbling over with animal spirits, they never will be conducted decently."

Hostility towards "foreign dance" has persisted into modern times. A Clare set dancer recounts how at a Gaelic Athletic Association (GAA) céilí in 1950, he and his party, who were dancing a Clare Set, were asked to leave the floor and the music was silenced until they complied.[7] At a céilí in the Mansion House in Dublin, the well-known traditional step dancer, Paddy Bán Ó Broin, and his partner, Máire Áine Ní Dhonnacha, a far-famed sean-nós singer and a native of Connemara, were ordered off the floor for daring to dance the Johnny – a Connemara version of the Highland fling or scottische.[8] The céilí dances still survive at dances organised by the Gaelic League's Céilí Clubs and are taught at the numerous Irish-language summer schools in the Gaeltachtaí. In some areas of Northern Ireland, they are seen as a badge of nationalism although, again, they are danced only at organised céilís and not at informal house dances. In the latter, the sets and half-sets and other nineteenth century couple dances, such as the Highland (fling), the barndance and the polka are still the vogue.

One of the basic tenets of the Irish language movement since the turn of the twentieth century had been "Ní tír gan teanga" which can be rendered as, "A nation without its own language simply does not exist." This dictum was seen as crucial to the construction of a national ideology in post-Civil War Ireland (the 1920s), and it presented the newly emerged national leadership in the southern state, who were "instinctively conservative" and politically insecure,[9] with a complex of problems. There had been no indigenous elite culture in the Irish language since the collapse of the old Gaelic order in the seventeenth century, and the twentieth century survival of so-called native speakers of the language was almost exclusively among economically and socially marginalised, impoverished small farmers,

7   Larry Lynch, Set Dances of Ireland: Tradition and Evolution (Miltown Malbay, Co. Clare: Séadna Books, in collaboration with Dal gCais Publications, 1989), p. 18.
8   Paddy Bán Ó Broin, Ceol Tíre 32, p. 14.
9   E. Rumpf and A. C. Hepburn, Nationalism and Socialism in Twentieth Century Ireland (Liverpool: Liverpool University Press, 1977), p. 75.

fishermen and labourers in "disadvantaged areas", mainly along the western seaboard. These people had an oral culture which was extraordinarily rich and complex but which reflected a world view quite at odds with the agenda of the new middle classes. Where these last sought the descendants of high kings and Ossianic bards, they found instead an embittered peasantry and rural proletariat with a long tradition of agrarian unrest and agitation, who were distrustful of all authority and whose music[10] and dances appeared wild and uncouth.[11] The popular style of singing in Irish later dubbed *sean-nós*, with its perceived strange intonation and timbre, was not broadcast on the national radio station to any significant degree until the 1960s. Until then, songs collected from *Gaeltacht* singers were broadcast using arrangements in conventional European harmonic style for trained singers with piano accompaniment.

The attention paid to dance was particularly severe. A further attempt to sift "alien" from "native" dance was set in train with the establishment in 1929 of *An Coimisiún Le Rinncí Gaelacha* (The Commission for Irish Dance). A reading of the minutes of the commission's meetings during the early 1930s indicates that there were many problems in achieving their expressed desire to exercise control over the world of Irish dance. The most dramatic development was the refusal of many of the Cork dancing societies to abide by the commission's demands. Since Cork city had been, for decades, a centre for excellence in step dancing, the commission's failure

---

10   "Our country musicians are possessed of the talent of music and have in their minds the idea of the beautiful in it, but they cannot reproduce them, for they lack the technical means of doing so (applause). Were they reasonably educated they would produce a race of musicians worthy of our history. Again, we had those who believed that Irish music should be rendered in scales of unusual construction. Many scales existed in ancient times but, alas, those who could teach us have gone. Because a singer or player, through lack of technical means, sang or played with a total disregard of any correctness of intonation, that did not qualify them to claim that they were using a scale of unusual construction. The majority of them did not adhere to the accepted musical scale, not that they used any other form of scale, but that their ear being totally untrained, they involuntarily produced a music not in any one scale, but in an infinity of scales of impossible construction (laughter and applause). Mr Darley then gave his violin recital of Irish airs." *Freeman's Journal*, 21 October 1908. (Darley was an arranger and composer who was deeply involved in the project of "recovering" Irish music.)

11   Alf Mac Lochlainn, "Gael and Peasant", in D.J. Casey and R.E. Rhodes (eds.), *Views of the Irish Peasantry 1800–1916* (Hamden, Conn.: Archon Books, 1977), p. 31.

to include them in its organisation was a severe blow to its aspiration to be a national body.

The commission's business was conducted as if it were a form of cultural court of law, with talk of "putting the case", punishment of dissident members by "sentences" of suspension: "six months reduced to one month", etc. Public criticism of the commission was forbidden, and we read of a registered teacher being reprimanded for writing to the newspapers criticising the commission. An insight into the thinking of the emerging organisation of *Cumann Na Múinteóirí Rinnce*[12] is provided in the following sequence of events, gleaned from the commission's minutes. The commission, at its meeting of September 1933, decided to bring some old dancers to Dublin to get the old steps from them so that they would be kept alive. A *céilí* was to be run to collect funds for this, and it was to be left to the commission to select the dancers. At the commission's next meeting, on 14 January, a letter from *Cumann na Múinteóirí Rinnce* was read. It stated that they would not subscribe funds to bring the old dancers to Dublin and, indeed, they condemned the proposal as encouraging "non-registered" teachers.

Already, the first dancing schools under the auspices of the Gaelic League had been set up in the 1920s with young children as pupils. The League sought to further tighten its hold on the field of Irish dance with its insistence that all dance teachers be registered. Their requirement that all teachers be Irish speaking ironically excluded the older layer of dancing masters who had attended school before Irish was on the curriculum. A canon of dances which were acceptably Irish was drawn up and published as *Ár Rincí Foirne*, the Gaelic League's dance handbooks, in 1939, and various movements and elements of style which were regarded as unacceptable were excluded. An account from County Armagh, in the northeast of the country, illustrates this latter process. Tomás Ó Faircheallaigh (Farrelly), later editor of *Ár Rincí Foirne*, accompanied by Miss Nan Quinn, a dance teacher from Dundalk, collected some group dances from older people in south Armagh in the early forties, a selection of which Ó Faircheallaigh published in the second booklet in the series (1943). The style of stepping of the Mullaghbawn dancers was not acceptable to the

---

12 Association of Dance Teachers.

Gaelic League choreographers, and the collector described the original dance as "*tuatach*" (crude, rough) and said, "*Chuir muidne snas air.*" ("We put a polish on it.")[13]

Later the dances were taught in a Gaelic League dance class in the nearby town of Dundalk where some young men from south Armagh learned the revised versions. When they brought this version back to south Armagh, it was severely criticised by one of the main original informants. The young lads' answer was, "Well, that's the way Farrelly taught it."

The exasperated reply was, "And who the hell do you think taught Farrelly?"[14]

It seems, from the evidence, that many of the Gaelic League codifiers were unaware of the existence of a vigorous, energetic and largely adult-male style of vernacular step dancing which had its roots not just in rural Ireland but also in urban areas such as the cities of Dublin, Cork and Limerick, Belfast, Derry, Drogheda, Dundalk and other major population centres. Even more to the point, when they witnessed a dancer from this tradition, they were quite simply unable to accept that this was Irish dance, in any sense.

A Gaelic Leaguer, in an article written on 30 July 1904, specially for the *Western People*, expresses this idea in typically uncompromising terms. He refers to:

> . . . a fine lightsome, nimble-footed display of the Terpsichorean art I witnessed lately. It was given, I'm told, by a Limerick man. It was not traditional, though, it was not Irish. It was pure music-hall dancing, just such as I saw given in Dan Lowry's about 25 or 30 years ago. This un-Irish style should not be tolerated. It is buck-jumping. It is fiercely vigorous, but in its execution there is no attempt at gracefulness; no attention to positions, of which the old dancing-masters told us there were five; there was little attempt at step – it was simply "jigging" or as sometimes called clog-dancing.

---

13 From a radio interview with the broadcaster Seán Ó Cuinn of Mullaghbawn, Co. Armagh.

14 Michael (Mickle) Quinn, Mullaghbawn, Co. Armagh. Mickle's father was one of Ó Faircheallaigh's original informants during his collecting-trips to south Armagh in the 1930s.

Another correspondent in the same paper on 27 August 1904 attacks the "spurious dancing" of the Gaelic League in Dublin as being "only a caricature of Irish dancing. The style is music-hall and barrack-room, Lancashire and clog."

He attacks Professor Reidy, whom he dubs "this self-styled Professor and Police pensioner from London", as being mainly responsible for this baneful influence. Reidy's dancing is also caricatured: "His acrobatic performance in the Rotunda [at the 1903 *Oireachtas* or annual gathering of the Gaelic League in Dublin] of what he called an Irish hornpipe was more like an exhibition of a flying-machine than Irish dancing."

However, Reidy himself was evolving an aesthetic which was critical of many aspects of vernacular step dancing. When, in the late 1890s, the London Branch of the Gaelic League had brought over the Cork dancers Willie Murray and Jack O'Brien, who were part of a long tradition of step dancing in that city, their performance did not please Professor Reidy, who had become the mentor of the London Gaels. Fionán Mac Coluim takes up the story:

Johnny Wayland [the founder of the Cork Pipers' club] asked me to find work in London for Willie Murray and Jack O'Brien, who were bricklayers by trade. This was easily done. They were wonderful dancers, particularly Willie Murray. I wouldn't say there was anyone in Ireland to beat them; but Reidy didn't like a lot of their steps particularly the "Salmon's Leap" and the "Drunken Man". According to him, they were "ungraceful" and "too acrobatic".[15]

Dancers such as Murray, O'Brien and Joe Halpin of Limerick (who was the Limerick champion of 1899 and who may even have been the target of the *Western People's* correspondent quoted above) would have regarded such criticisms as incomprehensible. Their tradition set a value on precisely those elements – involving an energetic, unashamedly exhibitionistic, highly competitive style of performance – which were being rejected by the new aesthetic of the Irish-Irelanders.

It is worth noting that the winners of step-dancing competitions had always been known as champions and that the coveted trophy of the

---

15 Fionán Mac Coluim's personal reminiscences. Unpublished. My translation from the original Irish.

urban dance tradition was a belt which closely resembled that worn by winners of boxing matches of the same period. Even the colloquial term still used in Irish for a session of step dance, *babhta rince* – a bout of dance – indicates the element of challenge which was never far from the surface.

The strength and vigour of this genre of dance with its unacceptably urban and working-class associations was classified as un-Irish, and we read in a report of the *Oireachtas* competitions of 1900: "The judges criticised the dancing very severely, as partaking of the Dublin stage-style rather than of the genuine Irish style of dancing."

Even in the west of Ireland the League found evidence of what they regarded as an un-Irish dance style. A commentator on the Mayo *Feis* of 1904 says: "In some instances there was a tendency to clog dancing and other displays more suggestive of English than of Irish style."[16]

Again in 1907, we find the *Oireachtas* prospectus obliged to state that: "in all the dancing Competitions the steps are to be genuinely Irish. Innovations such as Lancashire, clog and barrack-room dances being excluded."

The process of selection was relentless. It was also successful from the League's point of view. By the time the first dance schools under its auspices opened their doors in the 1920s, the style of solo step dance being taught was a modification of the old Munster style developed by the dancing masters of that region, and all other styles of vernacular dance had been consigned to obscurity outside their immediate geographical areas.

In all this talk of dancing and the controversies surrounding it, it is easy to lose sight of the fact that the League had been founded primarily to revive the Irish language. To this end, local organisers were appointed to conduct Irish classes throughout the country, but it was also their duty to spread the newly developed canon of Gaelic League *céilí* (group or figure) dances. For instance we are told that in Counties Meath and Cavan around 1917, the chief organiser was the poet Brian O'Higgins who "travelled long distances on a push-bike to carry out the good work". After the language classes he taught the new dances such as the Waves of Tory, the Bridge of Athlone and the Humours of Bandon. These "were popular for a few years – they were a novelty – but eventually they fell away".[17]

---

16   *Western People*, 11 June 1904.
17   James Argue (90), Copponagh, Co. Cavan, 1951, Irish Folklore Commission, vol. 1209, p. 584.

It is ironic that in this area of Cavan and Meath the old group reels – three, four and eight-hand – were the real local traditional dance. An old man of ninety called James Argue told the Irish Folklore Commission's collector P.J.Gaynor in 1951: "I would say that the three-hand and the four-hand reels were the oldest. They were danced in my father's time and before it."[18]

As late as 1927, Frank Roche of Limerick, the noted music collector, champion dancer and Gaelic Leaguer, whose father had been a professional dancing-teacher in Limerick, was lamenting the changes which had taken place since the League's involvement in the area of dance. He says:

> "It was unfortunate that in the general scheme to recreate an Irish Ireland the work of preserving or reviving our old national dances should have fallen largely to the lot of those who were but poorly equipped for the task. For the most part they were lacking in insight, and a due appreciation of the pure old style, and had, as it appears, but a slender knowledge of the old repertoire".[19]

One wonders what the venerable James Argue would have thought of the virulent condemnations of the group reels which had been danced in his area for generations as "alien" dance and "foreign interlopers" and the violent twists and turns of controversy on the matter which came close to splitting the Gaelic League, such was the sound and fury generated by the debate. His gentle and humorous turn of speech as documented by Gaynor suggests that he might have used the local well-worn saying: "All that bother and there's not a haet[20] about it now!"

---

18 Ibid., p. 576.
19 F. Roche, A Collection of Irish Airs, Marches and Dance Tunes (Dublin: Pigott, 1911).
20 Whit – as in not a whit about something. Not an atom.

Chapter Three

Learning to Dance

COTTER NA GRUAIGE (Cotter of the Hair) of Kerry, whose locks were as long as a woman's and who rode to his classes on a large white horse, the Giggedy Ryan of south Tipperary, Piccolo of County Cork (for that was the instrument he favoured), Máirín a' Rince (Máirín of the Dance), again of County Kerry, and Ducky Mallon of Belfast are only some of the extraordinary band of men and some very few women known as dancing masters whose exploits have left an indelible mark on the folk memory in Ireland.

The earliest reference we have to a dancing master is in a contract from an estate in County Cork. It reads in the original spelling:

An agreement made Between William Bayly, gentleman, of Ballincollig in the Barony of West Carberry in the County of Cork and Charles Stanton, dancingmaster, 21 of October 1718.

It is agreed that the said Charles Stanton shall teach the same William Bayly's children to the Number of four to dance until they perfectly Understand jygs, Minutes, Hornpipe and Country dances and such dances to dance very well as one of understanding in that respect shall Adjudge.

In Consideration thereof, the said William Bayly shall pay unto the said Charles Stanton the sum of 2 Gynies, or six and 20 shillings when taught perfectly as aforesaid and Not before. In witness thereof, the parties above named have Interchangeably set theire names and seales this day and year above written.[1]

This contract is interesting from a number of points of view. Firstly, it indicates that the ability to dance correctly was perceived as desirable in the children of a well-to-do family of the period. It also gives us an idea of the currently popular dance repertoire, and finally it points to an early application of the notion of payment by results, which must have been the bane of a dancing master's life if one of his pupils showed reluctance or, worse still, a natural tendency to have two left feet.

The employment of the dancing masters of the eighteenth century was by no means confined to the upper classes of the time. Arthur Young has left us many keenly observed insights into life in that century. He tells us that amongst the ordinary people of the countryside "dancing-masters of their own rank travel through the country from cabbin to cabbin with a piper or blind fiddler and the pay is 6d a quarter. It is an absolute system of education."[2]

The early dancing masters also taught "deportment" and attempted to impress upon their pupils the desirability of courtly manners and ball-room etiquette.

This aspect of the dancing master's art could leave him open to the satirist's pen. A leaflet, purportedly advertising an Irish dancing master's services and emanating from a printing house in Cheltenham in England, is headed "Attitude is everything", and goes on:

LARY QWILLIGHAN,
From Ballycockshusy,

Taches Dancing and the Greeces in all their extremities: includes the Leinster Cut and the Tipperary Fling.

---

1   JRSAI, vol. 18 (1887–8), p. 213. I am grateful to Seán Donnelly, Dublin piper and researcher, for the detail here.
2   Arthur Young, *Arthur Young's Tour in Ireland* (1776–1779) (London: G. Bell, 1892), p. 1446.

Young Ladies taught (gratis) "to cover the Buckle" and "the Step that cost his
Mother the Dollar."

N.B. Lary engages that his pupils shall never make a false step.

Elderly young Ladies taught to acquire ease and grace in all their motions, and
to rise and sink so as to beat nature out of the field.

N.B. Lary's the Boy.

P.S. Lary hears a Frinch Imposture is come to Chiltenham to teach the Ladies
Frinch steps, now Lary will shame him at any wake or fair in the Barony, the
spalpeen! and I am ready to fight him on the head of it, and glad to be asked.

Lary names his own terms, hopes the Leedies wont think them unreasonable.

N.B. I dance with a Munster brogue — Ladies taught the same.[3]

This type of heavy-handed humour was part of the armoury of the anti-
Irish "comic" tradition found in many British publications of the nineteenth century. The dancing master was but one target of this type of
stage-Irishry which was designed to raise a cheap laugh. Irish publications
of the period were kinder in their portrayal of the occasionally rather
eccentric figure cut by some of the dancing masters of the period. One
such was a Mr Tench of Wexford, whose teaching methods are affection-
ately described by a local commentator. He operated in the early 1800s
and "serenaded" a district of eight or ten square miles in the company of
a blind fiddler, canvassing for pupils, promising in his introductory speech
to turn out dancers who could "mingle with the quality as though it was
the next neighbour's child you had for a partner".

> [He] summoned the boys and girls of a townland to meet at some central
> farm stead, cheered their spirits with some gratuitous jigs and reels, and
> while their minds were gay, made out his list for the ensuing quarter of nine
> nights, each pupil to pay "a thirteen" to himself and a tester [six pence half-
> penny] to the fiddler. A compass of four or five townland thus completely
> filled the list of his disposable week nights, allowing Saturday for rest.[4]

---

3   I am grateful to Nicholas Carolan of the Irish Traditional Music Archive for bringing
    this publication to my attention.

4   Patrick Kennedy, "Irish Dancing Fifty Years Ago", *Dublin University Magazine:*, vol. LXII
    (1863), p. 430.

Mr Tench's insistence on using balletic terms, such as first and second position (of feet), "puzzé" (pousette), "Lépuzzet" (repousette?), is indicative of his desire to present himself as a man of specialised and arcane knowledge. It is fair to say that this emphasis on upper-class ballroom practice and semi-balletic terminology is designed to counteract the negative image of the rural dancing masters, whose living was often precarious and who were in many ways barely tolerated by authority figures such as the local clergy. Indeed, the practice of dance itself was often seen as suspect. In the locality and during the period in which Tench operated, we are told that:

> Very determined was the character of the faces set against the exercise [of dancing] by nearly all the Roman Catholic clergymen and some heads of families. Not that they were intolerant of relaxation on the part of the boys and girls, or supposed any evil inherent in the capering of the young fellows' legs more or less vehement, or the shuffling of the girls' pumps, half concealed by their long petticoats; but opportunities were hereby given for walking and talking with undesirable sweethearts, or sitting behind the assembly in unedifying proximity.[5]

Again, we are told that a well-to-do farmer would sometimes arrange private lessons during the day for his daughters and the children of some intimate neighbour rather than risk their mingling with undesirable elements. Thus, the objections to dance would not seem to be primarily moral but rather were designed to exercise a form of social control.

The arrival of the travelling dancing master in an area was the source of great excitement, for it promised not merely classes by day but dances by night for the pupils. There was great rivalry for the honour of putting him up, and he might lodge here with one pupil's family, there with the next. The classes were held in the winter months, from October to March. Whereas most of the dancing masters sought to enrol pupils for a term of tuition, thus guaranteeing a steady income, some charged per lesson or even per step.

In County Kerry in the late nineteenth century, in the parish of Keel, the people built a "long low house" for Jack Lehane, the visiting dancing master, and they covered it with scraws and thatch. In the winter and on the

---

5   *Ibid.*, p. 429.

Dancing in Youghal c.1930

Knockmonlea, Youghal, Co. Cork 1910

Street games, Co. Louth (Ulster Museum)

Kerry Dancing, Ventry, Co. Kerry (National Museum of Ireland)

Glenarm, Co. Antrim, 1904 (Bigger Collection Ulster Museum)

Miss Minnie Cunningham.

Charles & Russell
Belfast.

Minnie Cunningham, Belfast, c.1915 (Ulster Museum Collection)

Bangor boat 1906 (Ulster Museum Collection)

Strabane, Co. Tyrone, c.1910 (Cooper Collection, Public Record Office of Northern Ireland)

Tory Island, Co. Donegal (Colman Doyle)

Irish dancing, Aran Islands, c.1.910

For the above photograph we are grateful to Heritage House Inishere (Teachín Ceann Tuí), Inishere, Aran Islands and to the people who preserved it.

Siamsa Tíre

Siamsa Tíre

Irish dancing at Mount Morgan, Queensland, 1916 (John Oxley Library, Brisbane)

Irish dancer with piper Donald Mackay, at Mount Morgan, Queensland, 1916 (John Oxley Library, Brisbane)

wet nights, they used to dance in this house. "The dancing-master used get about £3 a month, for every pupil used have to bring him 4d every week."[6]

It was most unusual to find a female dancing master in the nineteenth century, but one such was Máirín a' Rince[7] who taught in a house in Baile Loisce in County Kerry in 1865–1870. The music was supplied by a local fiddler and Máirín's husband, Conchúr, collected the fee at the door. Máirín was a cracking dancer, it seems, as we are told: "*Ba dheas leat a bheith ag féachaint ar Mháirín ag rince in airde ar bhord*". ("It was great to see her dancing up on the table.")

The traditional Irish dancing masters were "of the rank of the people", as noted by Young,[8] and most were itinerant; that is, they travelled within a certain, often clearly defined geographical area in search of work. There were some dancing masters who were local but these were in a small minority. Generally, a dancing master had "no home of his own" and lodged with a local family during his stay, when the family concerned would have the benefit of extra (and free) tuition. Alternatively, he stayed in cheap lodgings in the area.[9]

It was the custom in many areas for the dancing master to hold a benefit dance for his pupils as a way of thanking them for their custom. An account from Knocknagoshel, County Kerry, tells us:

> We used to pay 10 shillings to the dancing-master and five to the fiddler. They'd give two "benefits" then – one after a fortnight and another at the end of a month. The dancing master and fiddler would bring a half-tierse of porter to each benefit. They'd buy it themselves for the lads. No one would pay anything at the benefit but spectators would come to the dancing some nights. They'd learn nothing but dancing around and they might pay half a crown but the scholars would pay nothing.[10]

---

6   Larry O'Brien, Annascaul, Co. Kerry, 1951, Irish Folklore Commission, vol. 782, pp. 299–300.

7   Also known as Máirín a' Dance. The detail here comes from Eibhlín Ní Mhurchú's account of dance in her native Kerry: *Ceol agus Rinnce Mo Cheantair Dúchais ó 1800–1880* Baile an Fheirtéaraigh: Oidhreacht Chorca Dhuibhne, 1990), p. 117.

8   Arthur Young, *Tour in Ireland*, p. 1446.

9   Martin Talty (piper), Miltown Malbay, Co. Clare, 1969, I.F.C. dance questionnaire.

10 David Walsh (92), Scairt, Knocknagoshel, Co. Kerry, June 1950, coll. Seosamh Ó Dálaigh, I.F.C., vol. 1178, p. 11

Occasionally, disputes could arise between dancing masters in an area if one strayed into the territory of another. Carleton says:

> The Irish dancing-masters were eternally at daggers drawn amongst themselves but as they seldom met, they were forced to abuse each other at a distance which they did with a virulence and scurrility proportioned to the space between them.[11]

Donncha Halpin, himself a dancing master in the Limerick area, told the collector Séamus Ennis in 1947 that there existed a kind of friendly rivalry between all the dancing masters which in a few instances became a deep jealousy.

> I have never heard of any instances where they heatedly opposed each other in any way and my only explanation of this is that their dignity prevented them from brawling with each other and the fact that they were fairly well separated in their locations. I have frequently been at contests between, say, a dancing-master from Shanagolden and another from Glin [both in County Limerick]; one would challenge the other and they would dance it out in public at some Sunday evening sports, frequently with no eventual decision.[12]

Stories abound of challenge matches between dancing masters. One concerns Din Moore, known as Mooreen, described as "the daddy of them all", who operated in Kerry in the late nineteenth – early twentieth century. "He beat a rival from the North of Ireland when each one had every second call for the music and every second dance and it was with Plúirín na mBan Donn Óg that he beat him."[13]

It seems that each dancer "called the tune" (that is, nominated a particular melody) and if his rival could not "follow the music" (perform steps which fitted the particular tune), he lost the challenge. Mooreen is still spoken of in awe in his native Kerry. "He was a genius. He'd think out a step while he'd be dancing."[14]

---

11   William Carleton, *The Poor Scholar* (Dublin: James Duffy and Co. Ltd, n.d., p. 168.
12   Donncha Halpin, Limerick, 1946, coll. Séamus Ennis, I.F.C., vol. 1304, p. 22.
13   Muiris Seóigh, Dún Chaoin, Co. Kerry, 1949, coll. Seosamh Ó Dálaigh, I.F.C.vol. 1168, p. 105.
14   *Ibid.*

Sometimes, rivalry between dancing masters would lead to a dancing contest at a fair. Puck Fair in Killorglin saw "five or six dancing-masters and two or three fiddlers playing for them, trying each other out and a big crowd around them".[15]

As is evident from these stories, most instances of rivalry were settled without any blood being spilt, although I have heard of cases where the encroachment of one dancing master into the territory of another or the alleged "poaching" of pupils led to overt violence. In west Clare, in the 1930s, I'm told, one dancing master accused another of canvassing for pupils in his area. The confrontation, initially verbal, could have ended in bloodshed as one of the parties had come equipped with a pocketful of large stones, having got "steamed" in a local pub. The aggressor was restrained, but the breach was never healed and the memory lingers to this day.[16]

One source of friction was caused by pupils changing from one dancing master to another.

> The new master knew from him what master he had left and he would often find himself the victim of harsh castigation on these lines: "What master were you with before you came here? . . . Well, go back to him for he has a bad job made of you and you want me to improve you. You're spoilt, I tell you. Why didn't you come to me first?"[17]

Whereas each dancing master had his own system of teaching and repertoire of dances, it is fair to say that, at any period, he would have taught the main solo dances based on the hornpipe, jig and reel and the group dances which were in demand locally, depending on the fashion of the time. The universally popular group dances which were the mainstay of the traditional repertoire – the two-hand, three-hand, four-hand and eight-hand jigs and reels – were passed on by the dancing masters. Where there was a dance craze, for example the quadrilles in the nine-teenth century, the dancing masters were not slow to respond and indeed

---

15 *Ibid.*, p. 247.
16 The names of the protagonists, though known to me, cannot be divulged for obvious reasons.
17 William Keane (piper), Mulgrave Street, Limerick, 1946, coll. Séamus Ennis, I.F.C., vol. 1304, p. 24.

were only too willing to graft on the new arrivals to the local repertoire. Similarly, the couple dances of the nineteenth century ballroom, such as the valeta waltz, the scottische (Highland fling), the barndance and the military two-step, were seen as being indispensable to anybody who wished to shine at a local dance. Dance fashion is no more susceptible to notions of political correctness than any other aspect of popular culture, and the idea which became current in the early years of the twentieth century that any dance could be seen as unsuitable because of its "foreign origins" would have been simply incomprehensible to the dancing masters, who lived by their trade of disseminating the currently popular dance trends.

The dancing masters generally began their course of lessons with the side step of the reel, which was an essential element in both the solo and group reels. Others preferred to begin with the "raisin" or rising step of the jig.

One teaching aid which was widespread was the fixing of a wisp of hay to the right foot and straw to the left one. In Irish speaking areas, they used "súgán" (straw) on the right and "gad" (withy) on the left. The reason for this practice lay not in the inability of the Irish to tell their left foot from their right – which some might, in truth, see as an over-developed national capacity. Rather it was because many of the dancing masters taught each step while facing the class and the pupils were thus obliged to learn in a mirror image of his stepping, which could be very confusing for beginners.

This little learning rhyme from Muskerry in County Cork illustrates the use of this learning aid:

> Come *súgán*, come *gad*
> Come *gad*, come *súgán*
> A*gus* hop upon *súgán*
> And sink upon *gad*.

This rhyme would have been sung to a jig rhythm.

Another jig-time fragment from County Kerry suggests that the dancing master's patience could sometimes be exhausted:

Agus síos sin Seáinín is suas sin Seáinín
Is greadadh chun do chos mar an deacair iad a mhúineadh.

(And up now, Seáinín, and down now, Seáinín,
Bad cess to your feet for they're very hard to teach.)

The dancing master would first demonstrate the step and then supervise the learning process by having the class practise the new movements. An interesting insight into the teaching methods of a dancing master in the early 1800s is given in the following account, which shows how he gave individual attention to each pupil, depending on the size of the class.

> The fiddler playing his best known air, and the pupil standing as far as the clear space allowed from the master, danced forward till they nearly met, the scholar making use of steps recently learned. He then returned to his place with backward steps, still facing the teacher, and repeated the operation a couple of times . . . The time devoted to getting through this programme depended on the number of pupils to be taught in the course of an evening. If the number was comparatively large there were but few repetitions, and the pupils were directed to practise hard before the next gathering.[18]

This dancing master taught steps which he called the "side step", the "heel and toe", the "pushing step", "cover the buckle" and the "upset and curl" or "spring and flourish". We are told:

> In one the mastery consisted in standing on the toes, and bringing alternately the sole of one foot over the instep of the other, in the quickest possible time. In another the fronts of the insteps were rapidly into contact with the backs of the legs. In the ordinary forward movement the front soles at a greater or less angle with each other, vigorously passed over the ground, the right coming immediately after and under the left one for some distance, and then taking the lead, and the peculiar twist of the body undergoing a change at the same time.
>
> The favourite "step" in hornpipes consisted of a vigorous shove of the foot in the air, a heavy slap on the floor, followed by three insignificant double beats, and then the passing over the duty to the other foot. Then the

---

18   Patrick Kennedy, "Irish Dancing Fifty Years Ago", p. 433.

side steps similar to the chassées in quadrilles must not be forgotten, in which, while the feet shuffled to right, the body swayed to left. The forward step and the set to partners in modern quadrilles were not known in their present slow style, nor would they have been practicable in the rapid movements of our rustic performers.[19]

The names for steps and indeed the steps themselves could be personal to an individual dancing master and unfortunately it is not always possible to decipher how they were performed. Generally, though, it is obvious that the teaching methods involved a progress from the simplest to the most difficult. A dancing master in County Cavan in the late 1880s began his lessons with the side step of the reel. Then came the single roll down, the double roll down, the winding step and the pupils finished with the hardest step, which he called the salmon's leap.

Donncha Halpin says that "the dancing-master first marched his pupils around the room to teach them deportment. He soon knew who would make good dancers." The first step that Halpin taught was the rising step of the jig which, he says, had the advantage of teaching pupils to balance on either foot. He also gives a detailed listing of the step elements of the local solo dance technique, which included the shuffle, the grind, sliding, skipping, drumming, the butterfly step ("jump off the floor with a twinkling of the feet in imitation of a butterfly's wing") and the double and single batter.[20]

The breakdown and codification of the step elements and the creation of new steps was one of the main contributions of the dancing masters, whose influence is still apparent in the performance of old-style step dancers in Ireland. Even now, a dancer from west Clare will say: "That step is one of Pat Barron's" or "That's one of Thady Casey's." In the Cork region, steps composed by a renowned local dancer called Freddie Murray, who operated during the 1920s and '30s, are named after him, and Joe O'Donovan, the wonderfully stylish dancer and dancing master of Cork, can perform all of Murray's steps. The great dancing masters of Kerry such as Jerry Molyneaux (pronounced Monnix) who taught in the early years of

---

19   *Ibid.*
20   Donncha Halpin, Limerick, 1946, coll. Séamus Ennis, I. F. C., vol. 1304, p. 11.

this century would all have composed steps, as well as handing on the repertoire of their district. A dancer called Phil Cahill of Tralee, County Kerry, who could dance five different "settings" or versions of the Munster solo dance "The Blackbird" learnt from Jerry Molyneaux, went on to become a dancing master himself.

Sometimes a step was seen as being inspired by a dream. The late Dan Furey, the noted dancing master from Labasheeda, County Clare, showed me a step called "Moore's Dream". "He had a dream and the dream came out in the step."[21] This step is still part of the repertoire of dancers in the Munster (southern) region. Halpin of Limerick is remembered in Halpin's Fancy and Halpin's rising step.

An individual dancer in the Munster area (Counties Clare, Cork, Limerick, Tipperary, Kerry and Waterford) may himself or herself "compose" steps by combining a number of suitable step elements, but generally dancers in this tradition tend to reproduce the movements exactly as taught by their dancing teacher. The notion of individual creativity was not encouraged in learners who were instructed by the dancing masters, although gifted dancers could put their own stamp on the prescribed steps.

One area in which there was a remarkable lack of unanimity amongst the dancing masters is their attitude towards male and female pupils. Some would not even allow girls into their classes, others taught different steps to male and female pupils, and still others had no fixed ideas on the matter and taught both males and females the same steps. In an account dating back to the early 1800s we are told that "Girls and boys learned the same steps, the only difference in practice consisting of the shorter and less lofty character of the steps when practised by the womenkind. The sole of the girl's slipper was never removed beyond three inches from the floor, while her partner, by way of variety, would give an occasional kick, as high as his shoulder."[22]

In a district where girls were excluded from classes, they often picked up the steps from their brothers or from male friends. The vast majority of dancers in the old traditional style of step dancing are of the opinion that

---

21   Dan so described the composition of this step to me during a field trip to Labasheeda in 1989.
22   Patrick Kennedy, "Irish Dancing Fifty Years Ago", p. 433.

female dancers are accepted simply on the basis of their skill, and the older performers all say that women dancers, though numerically fewer than men, were regarded as equals when it came to dance repertoire and excellence of performance. However, the dancing masters did not always take such a broad view. Donncha Halpin of Limerick had a particularly well-defined code of practice in relation to his male and female pupils. Certain step movements were deemed by him to be unsuitable for "ladies". He taught "more graceful" and "simpler" movements to his female pupils and based most of the girls' steps on the shuffle, whereas his male pupils used the more robust grind and single and double-drum.

A contemporary of Halpin's, Thady Casey, who taught in the neighbouring county of Clare, did not make any distinction between his male and female pupils. Thady had himself learned his dancing from his mother and passed on his steps to his own daughters as well as to his sons. His daughter Nellie, later Nellie Cox, taught dancing in west Clare and afterwards in England, where she settled.

A dance-teacher from Limerick called Margaret Murphy, who would have known Halpin and who also taught the old traditional style, said that the modern style is "only all hopping around and figures", and that men's dancing was "supposed to be harder but a good woman dancer could do his steps if she was able".[23]

The collector, P.W. Joyce, who conducted detailed research on dance for Petrie's *Ancient Music of Ireland*, tells us that "in Cork the women endeavour to emulate men in all the various and difficult movements, with few exceptions; while in Limerick, this for a woman, is considered unbecoming".[24]

Again, the idea of so-called "light" and "heavy" dancing did not correspond to "masculine" and "feminine" styles but rather was a matter of taste. Some dancers and masters maintained that dancing should be done lightly and artistically and that the grind, batter and drum should be executed with a very light touch, while others favoured a heavier and more "built" style with heavier beats in grinding and battering and drumming. In the modern era (post-1920s), when there was an enormous expansion in the number of dance schools and an ever-more bureaucratic

---

23   Margaret Murphy, Limerick City, 1969, I.F.C. dance questionnaire.
24   George Petrie, *Ancient Music of Ireland* (Dublin, 1855), p. 61.

system of rules and regulations governing dance practice, "lady competitors" who used the grind and Kerry batter were disqualified on the basis that these were barrack-room steps (in other words uncouth and unrefined and thus unsuitable for genteel young ladies). Even in the early days of Gaelic League involvement in dance, there was a perception in some quarters of the need for a purely "feminine" repertoire. A commentator writing in 1904 says that: "The double-jig was regarded as a dance for gentlemen for it distresses onlookers to see a gentle and demure young lady shaken to atoms by the vigorous execution demanded by this dance."[25]

Another element of dance style which was modified by the dancing masters was the use of the arms in performance. Early accounts tell of the dancing masters' attempts to deter "Paddy" from raising his arms and clicking his fingers, movements which were part of the earlier dance style and arose naturally in the course of an exuberant jig or reel. Indeed, accounts of "moneen" jigs in Kerry in the mid-nineteenth century confirm this use of arm movements. During the debates in the Gaelic League in the early 1900s on the authenticity of dance style, the question of arm movement was raised, so to speak. A "Special Correspondent" in the Mayo newspaper the *Western People* writes:

> Personally I am not inclined to favour rigidity of the arms as I lean to the conviction that the arms played an important part in old Irish dancing. I saw an old man dancing at a country celebration. His style was traditional if anything was. He was certainly a splendid dancer. His arms swung, rose and fell in rhythmic motion, and the effect was admirable.

Joe O' Donovan, the dancing master of Cork, who is still teaching, says that the older dancing masters used to weigh down their male pupils' hands with stones if they showed a tendency towards arm movements. As late as 1946, a woman from Limerick said that girls danced with the right hand on the hip in her young days and that she did the same until some adjudicator spoke against it.[26] It would seem that the tendency of some dancers in the Connemara *sean-nós* tradition to raise their arms to shoulder

---

25 *Western People*, 30 July 1904.
26 Margaret Murphy (née Maggie Mc Donnell), Thomondgate, Limerick, 1946, coll. Séamus Ennis, I.F.C., vol. 1304, p. 25.

height or even higher is an indication of the lack of influence of the dancing masters in this region.

The relative position of the feet was also a matter of preference in different districts. According to Halpin, the dancing masters of Cork favoured "close" dancing, where the feet were kept very close together when dancing, whilst in Limerick and Tipperary they favoured "loose dancing", a freer and more pliable style which gave the dancer the freedom needed to display his steps. It should be said that comments such as this might occasionally be coloured by the long-standing rivalry between Cork and Limerick and, indeed, echo the historic idea of the old dancing masters' sense of territoriality.

The spread of dance steps and styles can occasionally be traced through the influence of a particular dance teacher such as Freddie Murray of Cork, who was imprisoned in an internment camp in Frongach in Wales along with Eamon de Valera and others during the Troubles (1916–1921). While in prison he taught dancing to his fellow internees. Some of these men went on to teach in their home areas in the west of Ireland, thus spreading Murray's steps far afield. My own dance teacher, Annie May Fahy of Tuam and a sister of the renowned east Galway fiddler, Paddy Fahy, learnt her dancing from one of Freddie Murray's pupils and fellow-inmates, a man called Michael Coleman who was originally from Ballymote in County Sligo.[27]

Many dancers have detailed memories of their mentors. The County Meath dancer Tony McNulty, who was born in 1932, spent his early years in Manchester, where he learned step dancing from Frances Glynn of Galway. When he returned to Ireland, he got reel steps from Essie Connolly of Dublin, who was the founder of one of the first *Coimisiún* dancing schools, and he learned the "heavy" hornpipe from Harry McCaffrey who had a class in Parnell Square, on the north side of the city. Later, Tony's uncle Harry Fairtclough, the celebrated "museum-man" from Drogheda, took him to a local teacher, Bridie Mallon, who taught him an old version of the set dance

---

27 Annie May's sister Jenny (Campbell) was also taught by Coleman and won her first medal at the age of three. I am indebted for this information to Dr John Cullinane, the historian of the Irish Dance Commission, who has tirelessly traced the "dance trails" of these remarkable performers and teachers.

"The Three Sea Captains", in her house in Duleek Street, tapping out the steps on the shining lino laid over the kitchen's cobbled floor.

Not every dancer in the older traditional style has gone through such a formal and extended learning process, and indeed in many areas of the country such as Connemara, and in parts of the northern region including Fermanagh, Tyrone, Donegal and Cavan, there survive styles of dance which are not in any way influenced by the dancing master tradition. In the northern style, dancing was (and is) learned from a relative or from "going about". The noted reel dancer from Beleek, County Fermanagh, Paddy Magee, tells how he and his brother Johnny were taught step dancing in about 1936 by their uncle Johnny McGirl, who was around eighty at the time. He used to hold on to the back of a chair while showing them the stepping and demonstrated leg movements with his fingers "dancing" on the table while he lilted. A certain individual or family might be known as good dancers, and these would be a source of skill and reference point for learners. The concept of a formal class in traditional step dancing ("the old stuff") is non-existent. In the same way, a dancer in the old style or *sean-nós* of west Galway will pick up the elements of the local dance style in the home or in the community generally. When asked where she or he learned to dance, a Connemara dancer will always say, "*Phioc mé suas é.*" ("I just picked it up.") Dancers in the traditional styles of the north and west find the idea of a formal master-pupil relationship difficult to envisage and regard the notion of prescribed steps as anathema. The learning process involved in the northern and western styles could be compared to the procedure whereby an aspiring young singer in an area where the song tradition is strong will almost unconsciously absorb and mentally digest the distinguishing elements of the local style and will go on to practise and perfect the art through performance – whether private or public. Exactly the same process is followed by a dancer in an area where the transmission of dancing skills is more informal and takes place generally at a domestic level.

Within the context of the development of skills and repertoire, the contribution made by the dancing masters is immense and their names are legendary, but for sheer variety and entertainment value, it is hard to beat the story of Toby McCombridge from Cushendall, County Antrim, who operated as a dancing master in the early years of the twentieth century. He was born in 1884 in Cushendall where he later ran a small shop and did some barbering as well. He learned his dancing from a Henry McNally, living then in Belfast; McNally, however, was from the south of Ireland. Apart from "doing a little on the fiddle", he could whistle any tune. His favourite tunes for teaching were the "Harvest Home" for hornpipes, and the "Flowers of Edinburgh" and "Bonny Kate" for reels. He said, "They had great time and you could count the time and the dancer would have it correct."

He was a friend of the late Francis Joseph Bigger, a noted enthusiast of Irish culture generally, who used to ask him to perform at various functions and who got him appointed as a dancing master to a convent school in Sligo. Toby said, "There was one girl turned out a thumping good dancer from there."

He taught throughout County Antrim and also gave displays of dancing by invitation. He continues:

> One time Bigger came to Cushendall and wanted to know would I go to a "do" the Orangemen of Glengormley were holding. I said sure, so long as there was sport and fun and a drop of drink. Bigger had a lovely saffron jersey. He gave me that for the occasion and I came out and danced that way. I had knee-britches, of course, buttoned below the knee, and I wore long stockings and shoes. That was the rig.

When it came to a choice between running his shop and barbering business and taking part in dancing events such as *feiseanna*, Toby didn't hesitate. "Many's the time I closed the door and went off for a night or God knows how long. I was wild for the sport. Oh, I could have had thousands of pounds if I'd watched myself but what the Hell anyway."

Having moved to Scotland, where Bigger got him a job in a mill, he was conscripted into the British army during the 1914–1918 war.

During his training, he was stationed in Sheffield. "That was great. I met the Irish-English there." His reputation as a dancer became known. He used to take his shoes to the pub to replace his army boots so that he could display his dancing skills.

While he was in the trenches, filling sand bags to build the parapet, his pocket book, containing all the medals he had won for dancing, was stolen. They were never recovered. "It was a helluva quare drop to me, losing them medals." The collector Michael J. Murphy notes that, even after the passage of some forty years, Toby's eyes "ran quiet tears" as he recalled his loss. "I have cups at home; they'd be gone too only they were cups and I couldn't carry them."

After the war, his patron Francis J. Bigger got him a job on one of the Head Line boats sailing up the Baltic. They were ice-bound for six weeks at Riga. Toby says, "I had the best of fun and sport ashore." He met a Russian girl who would drive down to the ship for him in a four-wheeled sled pulled by ponies and they would "go here and there, dancing. I done the dancing." He recalls how she was "wild to go to England and wanted me to take her with me". This interlude ended when an ice-breaker freed their ship. After almost being drowned when their ship later ran aground in fog, he eventually reached home in Cushendall, where his mother persuaded him to give up seafaring.

We leave Tobias McCombridge, dancing master extraordinaire, in Molloy's pub at the corner of Tanyard Brae in the Diamond in Ballycastle, the town in which he spent his last years.[28] The world of dance had filled up his life and his story is surely a testimony to its power to shape the destiny of those extraordinary men and women whose skill provided such joy, both to themselves and to those whose lives they enriched by handing on the gift of their dancing. As they say in Ireland, *"Ní bheidh a leithéidí arís ann."* ("Their likes will never be seen again.")

---

28 Toby McCambridge (72), of Cushendall, in Co. Antrim, 1956, coll. Michael J. Murphy, I.F.C., vol. 1413, p. 290–7.

Chapter Four

Step Dance in the Irish Tradition

ENTRAL TO THE Irish dance tradition is the technique of "stepping", which involves a concentration on foot movements close to the floor in which the tempo of the accompanying music is beaten out by the dancer. The dancing masters who have operated within the tradition into modern times, particularly in the south of Ireland, could break down the flowing pattern of the dance into compact parts and define and name each specific movement within a step. Some of these movements have been given names such as the treble, the heel kick, the drum, the cut, the rock or puzzle, the shuffle, the batter and the grind. (See step appendix, p. 167.) Each step is composed of a series of these elements strung together to cover 8 bars of the music, whether jig, reel or hornpipe, the entire tune consisting of 32 bars. The hornpipe is seen as the dance which incorporates most of the step elements in the repertoire.

In the southern tradition, some steps are remembered as the creations of specific old-style dancing masters. Murray's No. 1 and No. 2 are called after the Cork dancer Freddie Murray, and his contemporary, Donncha Halpin of Limerick, composed Halpin's Fancy. The aptly named Moore's Dream is reputed to have been created by Denis (Din) Moore, who taught in west Cork and Kerry in the late nineteenth century. Other steps with fanciful names such as the Pigeon's Wing and the Salmon's Leap were also undoubtedly the creation of the older dancing masters. Many of these old steps are still danced by masters of the southern style such as Joe O'Donovan of Cork.[1]

Commentators often refer to the notion of the "dancing foot". This indicates not that the dancer is using one foot only in the step but that the main embellishments are carried out in the course of the 8 bars required to complete each step by first the right and then the left foot. The "doubling" or repetition of each step is a feature of the southern hornpipe, reel and jig tradition. So important is this element of the ability to dance each complex movement equally well using first the right and then the left as the leading foot that a dancer who cannot maintain the necessary balance will often throw his hat at it and abandon public performance. In this context, I was once trying to persuade a musician from Clare who had, I knew, attended dancing lessons in his youth to show me some steps. He refused, pleading, "I'd love to oblige, but the way it is, Helen, I have no left foot." I knew what he meant and left him in peace.

Where a dancer has learned to dance in a relatively formal master-pupil setting, she or he will tend to reproduce each step in performance as it was taught. In contrast, dancers who have learned in a more informal context will usually develop their own repertoire of steps from the step elements in their local tradition, and such dancers' performance will be highly individualistic.

Three main regional styles of stepping are still discernible today among traditional dancers. It is possible to identify a dancer as being from the south (Munster), the west (Connacht) or the north (Ulster) of the country. If there was a distinct style in the eastern part of the country, it has now disappeared.

The Munster Style

In the Munster style the most readily identifiable feature is the basic position of the foot in performance. The dancer is poised on the ball of the

---

1   See Joe O'Donovan's video, *Old-style Traditional Step-dancing* 1700-1930 (C180 VHS), issued by *Coiste Chorcaí, Comhaltas Ceoltóirí Éireann* – a tour de force of exquisite Munster stepping.

foot with the heel being raised about two inches from the floor. (According to Joe O'Donovan, the old dancing masters would place a piece of board under the heel of the weight-bearing foot of beginners to develop this practice.) The heel does not touch the floor except in the execution of certain movements, such as the drum. It is the mark of a bad dancer in Munster to allow the foot to step flat on the floor, and the dancing master would punish such a transgression with a sharp smack of a light stick on the back of the offending leg. The feet should be slightly pointed outwards, though not exaggeratedly so.

The Munster style forms the basis of the style used by the modern Irish dancing schools, albeit in a heightened, or as they describe it, a developed form. It also is the origin of the stepping to be seen in *Riverdance* and other stage shows since the choreographers and dancers in these shows are the product of the modern dancing schools.

The southern tradition has a larger repertoire of forms and tempos than the other regions. An accomplished dancer in the southern style would be able to perform the hornpipe, the reel and the jig as well as a brace of the intricate solo set dances such as "The Job of Journeywork" or "The Blackbird".

The double jig as a traditional solo dance has virtually died out in Munster where it is now regarded as a difficult or cross dance. The dance is in 6/8 time with the characteristic tempo

(The phrase "rashers and sausages" is often used as a mnemonic for this rhythm.) The name refers to the distinctive "double batter" or shuffle which is the main step element in this dance. The opening step of the jig is still the characteristic rising step or rise and grind, which was usually the first step taught by the old dancing masters, to the cry of "Rise upon *súgán*, sink upon *gad*." Each step is first danced "off the right foot" (8 bars) and is then repeated (doubled) off the left, covering 16 bars in all, or half of the tune. After this comes a series of steps, usually 3 or 5, each doubled (8 bars x 2 = 16 bars) and each a combination of the basic stepping elements of this style: grind, shuffle, cut, heel-tap, drum, etc. These are all danced in place. Formerly, in some areas of Munster, solo jig dancers separated each step with a 16 bar promenade in a circle, using a simple travelling step.

The single jig is also in 6/8 time but with the characteristic rhythm

It is faster then the double jig with more aerial steps and is named from its single batter. It is the dance typically depicted in early illustrations of Irish dancers and is probably the dance referred to by nineteenth century commentators as the moneen jig. As a traditional dance it is now extremely rare. In Clare it is known as "single time".

The Slip Jig in 9/8 time is now rarely performed by traditional dancers and is now confined to young female dancers in the modern dancing school style. It was a fast dance with steps very similar to those of the single jig. Between steps the dancers travelled around the floor using a characteristic slipping and hopping step, hence the name. It was also called the hop jig, and in some areas of the north it was known as the sling.

As in the jig, the single reel, usually written in 2/4 time, is faster and has the simpler steps, and is used to teach the basics to beginners. Many older musicians had tunes in their repertoires which they referred to as "old dancing master reels", and these all have the characteristic structure and tempo of the single reel.[2] The double reel, usually referred to simply as the reel, is slower to allow for more complex stepping. Usually written in 4/4 time, it is, in reality, more like 8/8, i.e. 8 quavers to the bar. The solo reel in Munster usually consists of a step for 8 bars made up of various combinations of stepping elements followed by a "lead around" (promenade) for 8 bars of simple travelling steps in a circle. This sequence is continued for any number of steps – usually up to 6.

The hornpipe is the main southern step dance, endlessly embellished by the Munster dancing masters. It is slower than the other solo measures,

---

2   Breandán Breathnach, *Ceol Rince na hÉireann* II (Dublin: *Oifig an tSoláthair*, 1976), nos. 111, 126.

allowing great complexity of steps. The dance opens with the lead out – forward for 4 bars and back for 4 bars. This is then doubled, as are all the steps in this dance, so each step covers 16 bars. Older dancers in Clare have said that the lead out was performed at house dances in order to clear a space for the dance. This opening was followed by any number of steps, once again made up of various combinations of step elements, such as the shuffle, cut, drum and puzzle. The usual number of steps performed was 4 or 5, but one Clare dancer – Anthony Casey, son of the noted dancing master, Thady – could dance 13 steps in a row, a major feat of stamina.

The last 2 bars of each step are known as the "finish". A dancer will often have a favourite finish for his steps, and some will seek to add to the complexity of the dance by devising a different finish for each step. Tradition tells of dancers who finished the whole dance with a final acrobatic flourish by leaping their own height in the air or by kicking the ceiling which, in the traditional Irish house, was made of wood and fairly low.

The final category of solo dance is the so-called "set" dance. The use of the term set dance in the Irish tradition is open to some misinterpretation since it is also used to describe the group dances based on the old quadrilles and latterly enjoying a revival. In that context, it derives from the French "suite de quadrilles" which became "set of quadrilles" or simply "set".

In the solo repertoire the term refers to specially composed step dances which the dancing masters "set" to specific tunes. These could be rhythmical adaptations of song melodies, like "The Blackbird"; popular songs of the day like the English "With Jockie to the Fair", which becomes in Ireland "The Jockey Through the Fair"; existing jigs, slip jigs or hornpipes or specially extended versions of these. Dancers refer to the first part of these dances as "the step" and the second, often extended part consisting of the complex step composition, as "the set". By and large, these dances are seen as the creation of the Munster dancing masters. "The Blackbird" – a set dance popular in Munster – is ascribed to a Limerick dancing master called Kiely who taught in the late nineteenth century.

Further confusion with regard to terminology occurs with the alternative name, long dance, being applied by commentators such as the noted music collector Francis O'Neill, to describe the set dances. His use of the term long dance indicates that the tune had a long second part of 12 or 14 bars, whereas the normal dance tune has two or more parts of equal length, with 8 bars each. Again the term long dance as used here is not to be confused with the old *rince fada* (long dance), which is a group dance and refers to the long lines of dancing couples with men and women dancing opposite their partners.

It would seem preferable to confine the term "set dance" to the solo dances which are "set" or inextricably linked to a certain "set" tune such as "Bonaparte's Retreat", "The Job of Journeywork", "The Blackbird", "The Garden of Daisies", "The Priest in his Boots", "The Three Sea Captains", "St Patrick's Day" and "An *Gabhairín Buí*". These dances form part of the repertoire of the Munster step dancer and were taught by the dancing masters into modern times. Many of them are still part of the repertoire of the modern dancing schools.

Occasionally solo set dances such as "Maggie Pickens/Pickie" in Donegal are encountered, but by and large this category of dance is confined to the southern tradition. It was not unknown in older times for some of these dances such as "The Drunken Gauger" to be danced by two dancers together or "The Priest in his Boots" by two or even four dancers. However, the impetus here would have been one of dancing solidarity or occasionally friendly rivalry. The dance remained essentially solo.

The Northern Style

In Ulster, the custom of two dancers performing opposite each other is an integral part of the step-dancing tradition. A dancer will invite another to join him by asking, "Will ye face me?" Dancers who know one another's dancing well, such as members of the same family, may dance similar or even identical steps, but generally each dancer will follow her or his dancing will. The Ulster dancer will most commonly dance a reel and when dancing a hornpipe will adjust the reel steps accordingly to suit the change in tempo.

Reel dancers in the northern style will dance a lead around, often holding inside hands; then they will dance two 8-bar steps opposite the other, lead around again, then a further 2 steps. Finally, the dancers "face the music" side by side and dance an 8-bar flourish to finish. A popular dance in the north is the "Maggie Pickens/Pickie", which is a form of crossed-sticks dance to a song tune of the same name involving a selection of heel-and-toe style steps. On Tory Island off the coast of Donegal, which is famous for its dancing, there is a special solo dance which is performed to the song "An Maidrín Rua". The dancer, Séamas Ó Dúgáin (Jimmy Mhary Willie), sings the verse of the song while standing in place and then does a lovely little side step movement to the chorus. The jig has died out in the north as a popular solo dance measure, though it is used for many group dances in the region such as "The Siege of Carrick" and the "sets".

As regards the solo step dance, the basic distinguishing element of the technique of stepping in the northern part of the country is the use of a constant heel-toe balancing movement by the foot not engaged in performing the distinctive features of a particular step. It is what could be described as a persistent drumming action which lends both balance and a subtle percussive intricacy to the dance. It is particularly noticeable in the solo reel. This heel-and-toe element is akin to that in English heel-and-toe dancing, which may account for its disapproval by elements in the nationalist Gaelic League movement in the early twentieth century.

A correspondent in An Claidheamh Soluis writes in 1904 of the northern style of step dancing:

> it is a series of "batters" – more batters indeed than the best Irish dancer would be called on to execute and the pity is that those whose wonderfully intelligent feet mistake the "clog" for the real article, should not have the opportunity of practising the real Irish hornpipe. The same remarks would apply to the jig as we see it danced in the neighbourhood of Dundalk [my italics].[3]

Evidence that this style of dance was practised elsewhere is provided in a report in the Western People, dated 11 June 1904, where a correspondent, reporting on the Mayo Feis of that year, says: "In some instances there was a tendency to clog-dancing and other displays more suggestive of English than of Irish style. These were few. In general, the dancing was characterised by gracefulness and excellence of execution."

---

3   An Claidheamh Soluis, 24 March 1906.

Occasionally, a dancer might perform in both the older traditional style and the more modern, modified Gaelic League style. In the 1930s, a dancer called locally "The Lordy Reilly" from "below Bailieboro" could dance both the "old and new styles". "He competed at *Feiseanna* here and there and he won every time. He was covered in medals."[4]

It is obvious from these accounts that the older style of dance described as "clog-dancing" persisted in many areas, particularly in the northern counties, and was ousted or in any case condemned as being un-Irish by the Gaelic League's insistence on a uniform style of "Irish" dancing devoid of regional variations. Where it has survived – as in Fermanagh, Leitrim, Cavan, Donegal and Tyrone – it is in spite of such disapproval. The northern tradition does not incorporate any form of organised competition for traditional step dancers. The arena for the dance remains domestic, or, at least, the performance takes place as part of a social event or function.

Unfortunately, there are very few dancers left who can perform in this style. Tommy Gunn, the renowned fiddler from Derrylin, County Fermanagh, can do "a bit of capering" as he calls it. There are also two brothers whose genius gives us an insight into why the Gaelic League commentator quoted above was so struck by the northern dancers' skill. Johnny and Paddy Magee of Roscor, Beleek, County Fermanagh, dance a reel in truly spectacular fashion. Because they are related, they have been able, over the years, to hone their performance and to work out a routine which will display all the elements of this dance style. The local steps are known as the side step, the heel-and-toe step, the slide step and the high step. Their routine is totally co-ordinated, and yet the casual observer may not be aware of this, such is the difference in their dance personalities. Johnny favours black, soft-soled shoes, and thus his stepping is barely audible, whereas Paddy dons a pair of strong, pale-brown boots which produce a diamond-hard sound. The spectator is conscious of the contrast in the two men's performing styles, and it is fascinating to see how the dancer's capacity to project himself makes such a difference to the audience's perception of the dance.

---

4   James Argue, Copponagh, Co. Cavan, 1951, Irish Folklore Commission, vol. 1209, p. 520.

Paddy remembers twenty men dancing a reel in Brallagh Hall – ten fa
ing ten. Each step was danced in place, interspersed with changing place
over and back and finishing with the high step which, as its name suggests, involves a kind of acrobatic high-kicking movement.

Very few young dancers are picking up this style of dance, but Johnny is
teaching his granddaughter Renate to do some of his steps, so there is a
possibility that this unique style will not be lost.

The Sean-Nós Style of Connemara

Another distinctive regional style which has persisted into modern times
is what is now called the *sean-nós* (old-style) dancing in the Connemara
Gaeltacht. This area would include the Aran Islands off the coast of Galway
and also a small but significant pocket in the *Gaeltacht* of Ráth Cairn, in
County Meath, in the east of the country, which was settled by people from
Connemara. In this style the reel dominates the solo step dance.

The Connemara style is characterised by a more flat-footed foot position than the other styles. Another distinctive feature is a movement
where the dancer uses the heel and the ball of the foot in a rapid rhythmical movement which has prompted some commentators to posit a link
between this style and Spanish *flamenco*.

The dancer in this style occasionally raises the arms to shoulder height
or even higher. Swaying movements of the body to left and right may also
be used. All nineteenth century accounts and illustrations of Irish dance
or "capering" indicate that vigorous arm movements were, at one time, an
integral part of the male dance. Arms were swung over the head with clicking of fingers.

In the following section I have outlined an analysis of some features of
the Connemara *sean-nós* style. The reader is encouraged to seek out live
performances in this as well as other regional styles. The visual impact of
the dance is, needless to say, essential to its understanding.

The most distinctive and characteristic foot movement in the
Connemara *sean-nós* style is termed *timeáil*. This percussive effect, which is
produced by using the heel, takes up 4 quavers or half a bar of the reel
and is the basic element in many *sean-nós* step patterns. Other typical
flourishes include:

Kicking the floor twice with the tip of either toe to the rear of the starting position in a rapidly repeated movement.

- Stamping with either foot in an emphatic fashion.
- A shuffling movement in which the ball of the foot brushes the floor whilst the dancer moves the foot forward and brushes it again whilst returning it to starting position. This movement is occasionally used by dancers in the Connemara region but is much less common than in the traditional southern (Munster) style.

Any or all of the movements detailed or referred to above may be used in any combination by an individual dancer. The repertoire of a dancer will not remain static and steps will be created as inspiration strikes, whether in the privacy of the dancer's own home or in the heat of a competitive performance.

The use of arm movements is, again, not fixed. Some dancers maintain the arms by the sides where they move slightly as the body changes position. The use of flamboyant arm movements, where arms are raised to shoulder height or even higher, is relatively rare and is used more commonly by male dancers.

It is hoped that my analysis of some of the techniques involved in Irish step dancing has been helpful to the general reader. In the future, detailed dance notation systems such as Labanotation will undoubtedly be used in this type of work. However, this elaborate and painstaking system is incomprehensible to the general reader, and it is hoped that the appendix will aid in the process of unravelling the dance and will give some pointers to those interested in finding out what on earth the flying feet are doing.[5]

Again, my advice is go and seek out the dancers, watch till you can follow some of the movement patterns, and then ask a dancer to show you a step or two. This is, after all, how the majority of traditional dancers have themselves begun to dance. You will find them more than willing to help you to find your dancing feet. In the words of the late Din Joe: "Take the floor, big, little and small!"[6]

---

5   The reader's attention is drawn to the ground-breaking publication, Michael Tubridy, *A Selection of Irish Traditional Step Dances* (Dublin: Brooks Academy, 1998), which notates ten step dances from Clare using a system devised by the author.

6   The catch phrase of the presenter of a popular radio programme in the 1950s, which featured group and solo dance; known colloquially as "Dancing on the radio".

Chapter Five

"That You May Live Till the Skin of a Gooseberry Makes a Coffin for You!": The Solo Dance Tradition

The two of us were sitting now, a good coat of sweat on us, a couple of sets being danced on the floor. A short, sharp-eyed, hardy block of a lad came in through the doorway. He stopped and looked around. Everyone was watching him till the dances were over. Then, he ran across to the musician, put a whisper in his ear and took a goat's-leap back into the middle of the floor. The musician struck up a hornpipe and the dancer beat it out faultlessly. It is wonderful feet he had, not a note of the music did he miss, as straight as a candle, not a stir of his body except down from the knees. The whole company sat watching him, without a word. You could hear them drawing their breath. He gave the last kick, looked around and cried out: "The broom from Maurhan you have seen. Who else will beat a step so clean?" No one answered. When he saw no one was rising to accept his invitation to beat a step with him, he disappeared through the doorway.

THIS EXTRACT FROM Muiris Ó Súilleabháin's book *Fiche Bliain ag Fás* [1] (*Twenty Years A-growing*) tells of a wedding celebration in Dún Chaoin, County Kerry, in the 1920s and describes the electrifying effect of the dancer's performance on the company. The solo dance tradition in Ireland is essentially a virtuoso affair. The purpose is to amaze, to intrigue, to invite wonder and respect. In a word it is exhibitionistic. Even in informal situations there is an underlying element of competition, of rivalry, of the throwing down of a choreographical gauntlet.

"When I was young, I used to think, 'Dancing is like fighting.'" This youthful memory is from the writer Dara Ó Conaola, who grew up on Inis Meáin, Aran, and it encapsulates this element of the solo dance tradition which surfaces occasionally, sometimes spontaneously and sometimes in a more organised fashion.

Dancing at fairs was widespread, and as early as the late 1600s the English traveller James Dunton describes a dancing competition at a fair in Drumconrath, County Meath, where the prize was "a bag of sneezing and a pair of broogs".[2] Two hundred years later, the practice was still going strong, as this account of dancing at a fairday in Sneem, County Kerry, shows:

> On the square of the town a number of large wooden doors were laid out side by side on which the dancing competition was held. It was the last time that Morty O'Moriarty adjudicated. He called out the names of the parishes and competitors, specifying the order of the dances. On his maximum of 100 "tips" we were surprised to hear the large number who were marked up in the high nineties. The final decision was accepted without a murmur of complaint, a tribute to the honesty and efficiency of the Glenbeigh dancing-master. The cheers and shouts for the victors waked echoes in the amphitheatre of surrounding mountains. Morty worked from a dozen outposts in South-West Kerry, of which Cahirdonal was one. Those who were competent to judge said he had no equal as a teacher. He chalked the kitchen floors in oblongs and taught the most difficult traditional dances. Part of his duty on Sundays was to determine and mark off the parish champions, and on fair-days and pattern days to pronounce among inter-parish competitors.[3]

---

1   In the original Irish, *Fiche Bliain ag Fás* was first published in Dublin in 1933. The English translation was first published in London in the same year. This edition republished in The World's Classics (London: Oxford University Press, 1972), p. 211.

2   In an appendix to Edward MacLysaght, *Irish Life in the Seventeenth Century: After Cromwell* (Dublin and Cork: 1939: 1950), p. 168.

3   Patrick Logan, *Fair Day* (Belfast: Appletree Press, 1986), p. 134.

Occasionally, rival dancers would challenge one another to a form of endurance test, and such an event could become part of the folk memory in an area. One such account comes from County Cavan:

> They used to tell about a peculiar dancing competition that was held eighty or ninety years ago at Mullinacross, near Kingscourt. A boon of fellows were coming home one night from Kingscourt, among them being "Little" Larry Farrelly, of Corraveelis and one of the Gargans of Copporagh. There was a heavy fall of snow at the time, but there was a flat stone in the surface of the road at Mullinacross that snow was never known to lie on – it would form in a high ring round it. Every man in the party had a pint or a half-pint of whiskey – it was cheap and plentiful at the time – and when they came to this stone there was a challenge between Gargan and Farrelly as to which of them could dance the greatest number of steps. The party sat down on the ring of snow, and the competition started on the stone. One man danced six different steps and the other man went out and danced twelve. They went on like that till Gargan had thirty-six different steps danced. Farrelly came along and didn't stop till he danced a total of forty-two steps. Gargan went out, but he didn't move a foot – he couldn't think of another step. Eventually, Farrelly says to him, "I dare you to make another step. If you do, I'll double the number I made." Farrelly won, but I don't know if there was a bet or a prize over it. The party sat down on the ring of snow and drank the whiskey and when they had it drunk, they started for home.[4]

The practice of dancing endurance tests is satirised in Flann O'Brien's account of dancing at a *Feis* in the fictional *Gaeltacht* of Corkadoragha.

> Eight more died on that same day from excess of dancing and scarcity of food. The Dublin gentlemen said that no Gaelic dance was as Gaelic as the Long Dance, that it was Gaelic according to its length, and truly Gaelic whenever it was truly long. Whatever the length and time needed for the longest Long Dance, it is trivial in comparison with the task we had in Corkadoragha that day. The dance continued until the dancers drove their lives out through the soles of their feet and died during the course of the

---

4 James Argue, Copponagh, Co. Cavan, 1951, Irish Folklore Commission, vol. 1209, pp. 537–9.

Feis. Due to both the fatigue caused by the revels and the truly Gaelic famine that was ours always, they could not be succoured when they fell on the rocky dancing floor and, upon my soul, short was their tarrying on this particular area because they wended their way to eternity without more ado.[5]

Dancing contests associated with ritual, whether religious or linked to pre-Christian practices, are well documented. Dancing for prizes at patterns was widespread. However, the most fascinating and detailed reference to dancing contests as part of folk custom and belief is contained in Máire Mac Néill's book, *The Festival of Lughnasa*. Based on accounts collected by the Irish Folklore Commission in the 1940s and '50s, the work throws light on the practice of festive assemblies on heights or at lakesides on a Sunday in late July or early August known as Bilberry Sunday, Garland Sunday, Lammas Sunday or Men's Sunday in various areas. An account of this practice from the Playbank, County Leitrim, tells us:

They made the ascent in the early afternoon and stayed on the mountain for several hours. The old went, as well as the young. Fiddlers and flute-players were there to play for the dancers. As at all other mountain assemblies, the dancing was not of the kind that all joined in but rather, performances by small numbers of gifted dancers. There was keen competition and appreciation. Fame was assured after a good performance on the Playbank.[6]

In an overview of the reports we are given an impression of the pervasive nature of the custom in rural Ireland and the central role of the dance competitions therein:

Dancing on the heights was spoken of in almost all reports. Specially worth remembering are the custom of selecting the best dancing couple at Drury Hill and Cnoc na dTobar in Kerry, the choice of bride as prize for the best dancer at Ganiamore in Donegal, the dancing competitions on the Playbank Mountain in Leitrim and the dances which led to fights at Caher Roe's Den on the Blackstair Mountains and at Ardevin on Slieve Bloom.[7]

---

5   Flann O' Brien, *The Poor Mouth* (London: Hart-Davies, 1973), pp. 58–9.
6   Máire Mac Néill, *The Festival of Lughnasa* (London: Oxford University Press, 1962), pp. 181–2.
7   *Ibid.*, p. 423.

So, not alone was there rivalry between dancers, but sometimes, "fac tions backing champion dancers were liable to fall out and fight".[8]

Dancing on a height was a common feature of a spontaneously occur-ring bout of rivalry at a house dance. The half-door would be taken off its hinges and placed on the floor for the first round of dance, and if a winner did not emerge, the door was then placed at increasing heights – on top of a table, then on a barrel placed on the table – until one competitor either balked or fell off. One account from Kerry tells of competitors danc-ing on a soaped wooden board. If no one was the winner first time around, a smaller soaped board would next be placed on top of this. Needless to say, the eventual victor required not only dancing skill, but also balance, agility and sheer nerve.

In a wonderful account of such an informal dancing competition, a farmer from Curraghboy, near Athlone, County Westmeath, tells us:

Step dancing was a great go in the old days and the old men and women who were the dancers followed the music. When the step dancing was going to start, there was a shout; "Take down the door!" The kitchen door was then taken off the "buckans" and left on the floor and each dancer jumped on to the door one after the other till one was declared the winner. About 80 years ago in this part of the country they could not decide the winner. Then the door was put up on the table but still no winner and at ten o' clock in the morning one man won the contest by dancing a reel on the door on top of the chimney of the house.[9]

The response of the onlookers often served to urge on the dancer. Shouts of "Some can do it but you know how!", "It's a pity you'd ever grow old!" or even, we're told, "That you may live till the skin of a gooseberry makes a coffin for you!" from County Cavan, would rend the air. In Clare, the shout was the economical but much-coveted "Style! Style!" High praise indeed from an area steeped in dance skills. In Connemara, the dancer would be urged on by the cry: "Faoi do chois!" (Rise it!). Occasionally, the fun involved the urging-on of an unskilled dancer who pounded the

---

8   Ibid., p. 172.
9   Thomas Kelly, 1969, I.F.C. dance questionnaire.

...oor without any finesse, but generally, a poor dancer would know better than to subject himself to ridicule, unless the drink was in and the music provided an irresistible urge to hoof it.

Some dancers had special party tricks. For instance, a Michael Tully of Bailieboro, "could dance and play the fiddle at the same time and he could dance with a partner and play the fiddle behind her back while he'd be swinging her around the floor. He was a real comedian. Sometimes when he'd be dancing at a concert or a social gathering, he'd make faces at the audience."[10]

Comic or grotesque dances were also highly popular at a time when notions of political correctness were not a consideration. The dance song "Nóra Chríonna" provided a suitably bawdy vehicle for such performances with verses such as:

> Corraigh do thón a Nóra Chríonna
> Is féach cad a gheobhair i gcomhair na hoíche
>
> (Waggle your bum, Nóra Críonna,
> And see who you'll get for the night.)

or

> "Come under a bush," a deir Seán Ó Fianna.
> "And what for?" says Nóra Críonna.
> "For a scaitheamh," a deir Séan Ó Fianna.
> "Rub sand off yourself," says Nóra Críonna.

"When they'd be dancing it they'd twist and shake their bodies and do funny things like that that would cause great amusement."[11]

Apparently, similar contortions also accompanied the tune "Sporting Paddy" in this area of Cavan. It is worth mentioning that the words of many dance songs are unfit for delicate ears. When I was young the dogs in the street knew the verse beginning "My Auntie Mary had a canary" (to the tune of "The Cock of the North") and we would sing it at the top of our voices, delighting in the shock waves it produced among the grown-ups in our lives.

---

10   James Argue, I.F.C., vol. 1209, p. 523.
11   Ibid., p. 606.

A particular category of virtuoso solo dance is what could generally be described as crossed-stick dances. Here, the dancer's skill is tested by his or her ability to dance intricate steps while negotiating a "grid" produced by various trappings. In some instances, as for the "Maggie Pickie" in Donegal, which I collected from Breandán Bonnar of Na Glaisigh and which he had learnt from his grandfather, Aodh Coll, in the 1930s, crossed sticks were used. Otherwise, a cross pattern could be produced by burning a stick in the fire and marking the floor with it. When I recorded him, he was using tightly rolled crossed handkerchiefs. In other areas, a belt or a spade handle were used. Sometimes, as in the "Gabhairín Buí" in Clare, crossed brushes or sticks were used. Junior Crehan of Clare told me that occasionally a fiddle would be put down on the floor, which indicated an amazing faith in the skill of the dancer. This type of dance is found countrywide and is sometimes known as the Step of Cipín, the Rince an Chipín, the Peadar Ó Pí or the Pater-o-Pee. An old description of this last dance is found in an account in 1850 by an Anglo-Irish gentleman. In a "hovel" in Mayo, his hunting party is entertained by local dancers and musicians:

> One gentleman alone was standing. Presently two sticks were laid crosswise on the ground, the piper struck up an unusual sort of jig and the feat commenced. "This," said my kinsman, "is called the Pater-o-pee and none but an accomplished dancer would attempt it." To describe the dance would be impossible; it consisted of an eternal hopping into the small compartments formed by the crossing of the cudgels on the floor, without touching the sticks.[12]

As regards technical skill, a good dancer in the tradition was described as "very sweet on the feet", "as loose as a hare" or, it was said, "You'd go to the butt of the wind to see him dancing." Concerning one dancer's opinion of another, I remember once being somewhat taken aback when I commiserated with a dancer from Clare soon after the death of a fellow dancer whom I had recorded some years previously. Quick as a flash, he shot

---

12 William Hamilton Maxwell, Wild Sports of the West (London: E.P. Publishing, 1973, reprint of 1850), pp. 79–80.

back: "Divil a pity. Sure the whore hadn't a shtep in his leg!" Generally, dancers will avoid such uncompromising judgements and most will be kind to the less gifted. One of the most memorable and deeply felt compliments I ever heard comes from the Cavan dancer, Tom King, who said, after he first saw the Mullagh, County Clare, set dancers, led by the indomitable Ollie Conway: "Mighty dancers! If they had fifty legs, they'd use every one of them!"

The old-style step dancer will generally dance within roughly one square yard. A traditional dancer performed "in his tracks". There was no attempt at what one dancer described as "skating around" as in modern dancing. It was said of good dancers in the old style that they could "dance on a plate" or even – the highest accolade – "on a sixpence". These accounts indicate that an ability to dance "in place" was highly regarded. A dancer in the old style who was clumsy or awkward and tended to lose control was said to be "killing clocks" (stamping on black beetles). Another unflattering term for a bad dancer was a "rat killer". An observer of bad dancing was once heard to comment, "That fellow should go to the vet and have his hoofs pared."

The old-style dancer holds the hands loosely at the sides with the backs of the hands facing forward. The body position is erect but not rigid. Older people would say that the perfect dancer moved only his legs and his feet, not his body. There wasn't much thought of a dancer that allowed his body to shake and bend and swing. Some dancers had that failure, as they saw it.

The traditional step dancer wears no particular style of footwear. A pair of good leather-soled shoes is favoured as these help to accentuate the sound pattern of the dance, although some dancers prefer soft-soled shoes. However, within living memory special footwear was not unknown. The use of clogs for dancing is a case in point. Captain Francis O'Neill, writing in the early twentieth century, sometimes referred to hornpipes as "clogs": "A tidy clog brought to Chicago many years ago by Bernard Delaney, our celebrated Irish piper, became a great favourite, especially among the dancers."[13] Later he discovered that this tune was known in Ulster as "The Londonderry Clog".

---

13   Capt. Francis O'Neill, *Irish Folk Music: A Fascinating Hobby* (Chicago, 1910), p. 119.

An elderly man from County Cavan tells of how in former days (*c.* 1880)

... the men wore clogs when dancing. The clog-maker generally made them for the purpose. They would be left by and only worn whenever there would be a dance. There were boot-clogs and shoe-clogs. I heard the clogs were easy to dance in. There was plenty of clog-dance long ago. The girls wore either shoes or boots or clogs. You'd see girls them times doing step-dance and them wearing clogs.[14]

Even in an area such as County Galway which is not usually associated with this, there are accounts of clog dancing. For example, in 1937, a local man, Tom Carty of Ballymore, County Galway, "made clogs to order and it's well Tom could time the tune with his clogs".[15]

I have come across several references to clog dancing in Dublin at the turn of the century. For instance, the writer Seamus Fenton recounts how he met a hurdy-gurdy man in Roscrea who had worked in a pub in Capel Street in Dublin in the early 1900s. His "pal was an expert clog-dancer who, with Bill Lobster, gave exhibitions to customers in a backroom of the same old tavern". Fenton also mentions that "the glory of the old Dublin of clog-dancing, cheap porter and fine ballad-singing was vanishing fast".[16]

A man from Kerry describes how, in the early 1900s, he saw dancing shoes made from the skin of a dog. The sole was made from ordinary leather but the uppers were of dog skin. "They'd tighten them on their feet with thongs of leather."[17] He also mentions what he calls "perka" shoes (*bróga peirce* was the Irish version), which appear to be similar to the gutties or sandshoes which are still manufactured. The name "perka" would seem to derive from the Anglo-Indian "gutta-percha" – a form of rubber.

There are occasional accounts of step dancing with silent feet, as in the contemporary Scottish Highland style. Mooreen, a Kerry dancing master from around the turn of the century, liked to display his steps by dancing on a table in his socks. "He wouldn't break an egg under his feet." Another

---

14 James Argue, I.F.C., vol. 1209, p. 541.
15 Kathleen Hurley, Corlock House, Ballymore, Co. Galway, 1938, I.F.C., vol. 3, p. 22.
16 Seamus Fenton, It All Happened (Dublin: M.H. Gill, 1948), p. 330.
17 David Walsh (92), Scairt, Knocknagoshel, Co. Kerry, June 1950, coll. Seosamh Ó Dálaigh, I.F.C., vol. 1178, p. 5.

trick of Mooreen's was to arrange the fire-tongs under the table in such a way that "when he was tipping the table with his feet the tongs was tipping the floor". Sometimes he would put a pan of small stones under the flag he was dancing on so as to accentuate the sound pattern of the dance.[18] Even heavily built men sometimes favoured a "light" style of dancing. One such was a dancer called Sullivan, from Knockbrack, County Kerry, who "used dance as light as any girl on the flag of the hearth and when he'd want to hit a clout on the flag you'd hear the echo below on the road".[19]

The older people in general had great admiration for the "lightness" of a dancer. She or he could be described as being "as light on their feet as a cork". A dancer called Mickey Lynch from Doon, County Cavan, could "dance a hornpipe and an egg tied to the heel of each of his boots and he wouldn't break any of them".[20] Again, a dancer from west Kerry says of the old style in the area that the lighter the dancer the better, and that the dance should be virtually noiseless "except that a quiver came in the music; he should time that quiver".

In a final reference to light or silent dancing, a curious account from the Aran Islands, in the early 1900s tells of men dancing a hornpipe wearing the traditional shoes of soft cowhide and holding short sticks. "Scarcely any noise was heard, as they can move quite silently on the pampooties or cowhide shoes which they wear, the quiet being broken only by the clanking sound of the sticks as they clashed."[21]

Some dancers in the old traditional style, however, felt happiest dancing in heavy footwear, usually the working or hobnailed farm-boots with their characteristic rows of nails on the sole and heel which would "knock splaincs [sparks] out of the floor". This style of dancing obviously involved making the maximum possible din. "When they'd be dancing they'd nearly put their feet through the boards . . . If they weren't making plenty of noise it was no good."[22]

---

18   Ibid.
19   Ibid., pp. 10–12.
20   James Argue, I.F.C., vol. 1209, p. 532.
21   B.N. Hedderman, *Glimpses of My Life in Aran* (Bristol: John Wright, 1917), p. 56–7.
22   John Cullen (75), Ardlow, Co. Cavan, 1951, I.F.C., vol. 1209, pp. 514.

Peter McArdle, the great fiddle player from County Louth, talked of a next-door neighbour of his who died in the early '40s. He remembers him dancing in his working gear:

He'd come in after a hard day's work there and get up on the floor after the tea and he'd just give the knees a couple of shakes and he'd kettle-drum that [tune]. He'd may be on his knees all day picking potatoes at a pit in the cold. It was extraordinary. There wouldn't be a movement – he'd put the hands down. You'd think he was concrete right to the knees.[23]

A dancer from Cavan called Nelson "couldn't dance unless he had a pair of strong boots on him. When he went to compete in Dublin [in the 1920's] he had to throw them off and put on a pair of light shoes."[24] Despite his unease in the lighter shoes, he went on to win the prize.[25]

Dancers tell of tricks which were used by competitors to achieve the desired sound effects. When the Irish Dance Commission banned metal tips on soles and heels in the 1940s, dancers would, I'm told, get an extra sole put on their shoes, wet it well and walk on a gravel road so that the tiny stones became embedded in the leather. When this dried, "you had a concrete-hard piece on your shoe and they could do nothing about it". Another dancer mentions rubbing orange peel on the wetted soles of dancing shoes to harden them. Sometimes, the sole and heel would be slit open and coins or weights would be inserted so as to emphasise the percussive sound effects.

Occasionally, a dancer who was particularly skilled might be given an honorary dance name. Amongst these are a dancer from Ventry in Kerry who was known as *Micilín na gCos* (Micilín of the Feet), and a noted dancer from Tipperary who was known as the "Style" Walsh, because of his stylish dancing. A dancer could be known by the name of his favourite tune. For instance, a dancer from Cavan was known as the "Swag" Murtagh after

---

23   Peter McArdle, Tallanstown, Co. Louth, coll. Breandán Breathnach, I.T.M.A.
24   John Cullen, I.F.C., vol. 1209, pp. 530–1.
25   A most unusual account of a prize for dancing is given by the dance teacher Mrs Margaret Murphy of Limerick. Her father, "in his young days" (c. 1880) twice won a dancing-contest organised by Duffy's Circus. The prize was £5 – a fortune in those days. In a letter to Breandán Breathnach, 1969.

"The Swaggering Jig" which he invariably requested from the accompanying musician.

A dancer from near Virginia, County Cavan, called James Tormey guaranteed his notoriety by announcing his performance with the following rhyme:

> Here is the way to caper
> And here is the way to prance.
> I came all the way from Ballinagh
> To teach you all to dance.

"He'd sing that while he'd be dancing the first few bars of the tune. Then he'd start off and dance side steps around the floor and then he'd start in earnest. He was a tall man and wore a long beard. At sixty years, he was as light on his feet as a man of twenty."[26] Tormey is reputed to have played the fiddle and danced a hornpipe along a table set for a wedding, dancing "through the cutlery".

Possibly, the highest accolade was to be known simply as the "Dancer". One such was William Wrynn from the town of Muff in County Cavan who was known as Willie the Dancer. An observer describes his performance at the fair of Muff:

It may have been about the year 1924 when I heard music and cheering coming from the yard behind McGovern's public house opposite the market yard. Inside I found that a door had been taken off its hinges and I pushed my way through the crowd and for the first time in my life saw Willie the Dancer. There were, as far as I can remember, about 200 people, mostly men, watching him and admiring his skill, and indeed, he was a splendid dancer. I do not know how to describe Willie's dancing but indeed I am glad that once in my life I saw a real expert traditional Irish dancer. As I try to recall that day I remember some of the crowd saying that Willie had won prizes in New York for his dancing when he danced on the stage there with "bells on his dancing-shoes".[27]

---

26 James Argue, I.F.C., vol. 1209, pp. 529–30.
27 Patrick Logan, *Fair Day*, pp. 134–5.

This account is an indication that gifted dancers could make a living from their skill. Following a performance at a fair or other gathering, a collection would be made for the dancer and the accompanying musician. In similar vein is the following description of a Waterford man's dancing exploits:

My mother's father was a great man for dancing and he used often spend days gone travelling with some piper or fiddler and then come home. Someone told him and he working in Ring digging spuds that there was a great piper after coming to town. The minute he heard that, he left spade and all there and put on his coat and made off walking for town. He met the piper and when some of the lads saw him talking to the piper they got a few boards and they nailed them together and they put him up on it and then the piper began to play. He was dancing "The Blackbird" and he was going ahead fine and a big crowd was gathering when they heard he was there and there was plenty money being thrown into the cap . . . They went around the town then and God only knows the money they made – my grandfather dancing hornpipes, reels and doubles and singles and the piper playing. They went on a big "booze" then, the two of them, and my grandfather didn't come back to the spuds for three days.[28]

Dancing was, obviously, a recognised means of raising money, but, as the next story illustrates, a dancer's skill might stand him in good stead in unexpected ways. It tells of a dancer in Cavan in the nineteenth century when most small farmers did not own their land but instead were obliged to pay rent to the local landlord:

He was a small farmer on the Pratt estate – Johnny M. of Copponagh – and one time he wasn't in a position to pay his rent. There was a couple of half-years rent owed by him. The poor man was at his wits' end when he hit on a plan. He made up his mind to go to Cabra Castle and make a personal appeal to Pratt (the landlord) for time to pay. Johnny got his stick and started on his journey at the "scrake" of daylight and when he landed at the castle the gate leading into the big yard was open. He "dodged" into the

---

28 Willie Curran (40), Ballinure, Dungarvan, Co. Waterford, 1936, coll. Nioclás Breathnach, I.F.C., vol. 259, pp. 662–3.

yard and he was waiting till he'd see some of the servants that would convey word to Mr. Pratt that he wanted to speak to him. While he was waiting one of the Pratt ladies began to play the piano inside in the castle and after a bit she struck up either a reel or a hornpipe. Johnny began to dance it and the more she played the more he danced. What happened, but another of the Pratt girls looked out and saw him dancing. In a jiffy there was a number of them looking out at him and old Mr. Pratt was called and he came and looked out at him along with the rest. Finally, Pratt had a message conveyed to him that he was wanted inside. A servant ushered him into a room and Mr. Pratt came in and complimented him on his lovely dancing. He asked him for his name and address and inquired what his reason was for coming there at such an early hour. Johnny explained the best way he could about so much rent being due, that he wasn't in a position to pay it, and that he came to ask his Honour to give him time to make it up. Pratt sat down at a table and got his pen and ink and wrote him out a clear receipt and told him to start in the new year and try and do the best he could in future. And he made the servants give him his breakfast before he started on the road back to Copponagh.[29]

That last story goes back to the early years of this century and has a certain folkloric, even epic, quality about it. It belongs to another era. The world of dance is, however, no respecter of the relativities of time and place, and when I went to talk to a dancer in north County Dublin recently, I was reminded that the commonplace of one generation can become the stuff of legends for the next.

Josie Conway, née MacCormack, now living in Seapoint, Balbriggan, grew up in Edgeworthstown in County Longford in the 1920s. Josie's parents loved music and dancing. Every Friday night saw a *céilí* in their home with half-sets being danced to beat the band in the big old kitchen with the flag floor. She remembered sitting crouched beside the range watching old Barney Reilly "who was never taught to dance at all but by God he could dance a hornpipe". He would swing his arms to the rhythm of the music during the last step of the dance and would raise them over his head in a triumphant gesture as he gave the final stamp.

---

29 James Argue, I.F.C., vol. 1209, pp. 517–20.

Josie, her brother Peadar and her young sister Sadie were taught dancing first by Ann Glennon of Longford and later by Peter Bolton of Dublin. They won medal after medal as a trio in the competitive world of Irish dancing in the 1930s until one day, out of the blue, a letter arrived from the proprietors of Duffy's Circus asking the trio to join their troupe the following summer season. Their parents were initially apprehensive at the idea of allowing their teenage children to join the circus but when the contract arrived, with details of strict supervision included, they relented. Thus began a magical time for Josie, living in a wooden wagon with marvellous devices such as fold-up bunks and a cosy little stove on which they did all their own cooking. The wagon was drawn along the byroads of Ireland by three well-trained horses driven by her brother Peadar. The tent-erectors, co-incidentally called MacCormack, would take down the tent after the show and set out for the next destination at three o'clock in the morning, and when the thirty-six-wagon company arrived the next afternoon, the big top would be ready and waiting.

It was during the war years and, as Josie said, it was hard to get many foreign acts. Most of the performers were young, and they included Young Atlas, the strong man from Keshkerrigan in County Leitrim, and Elroy the Armless Wonder. The Duffy family themselves were all performers. John, James and Lily Duffy did the trapeze and Annie did the ponies and the horses. Josie, Peadar and Sadie were the stars of the show. Their Grand Finale began with a performance by the all-Ireland prize-winning Emerald Girls' Band, who finally thrummed and piped the MacCormack Trio on to the stage to the strains of "Let Erin Remember the Days of Old". Their show-stopping performance included the three-hand reel, with intricate steps and figures, and their own composition – "The Troupe Hornpipe" – which included every twist and turn of group dancing, combined with a spectacular display of doubles, trebles, cuts, rocks, passovers, dancing to left and right, and such spectacular percussive stepping as had never before been seen either under a big top or outside it. The musician they engaged to accompany them was an accordion player called Paddy Reilly from Ballinacarrigy in County Westmeath, an All-Ireland champion. Josie says: "He was fantastic. He'd put every step under your foot."

IRISH DANCE

People often talk about certain times of their youth as being the happiest days of their lives, and listening recently to Josie MacCormack Conway telling her story there in the industrial town of Balbriggan, with the Belfast train swishing periodically past her gateway, I was aware, as never before, of the truth of that notion. Josie is now getting on in years and suffers a lot from arthritis, but she showed me some of her favourite steps from a seated position in her favourite armchair. Her feet rose and fell, tapping out the routines she had shared with her beloved sister Sadie and her friend Tony McNulty and his sister Lil Murphy – all of them now dead and gone – who had been part of her world of dance, conjured up so generously and so vividly in her living room that bright March morning. I felt privileged to be there, to listen to her talking and to be reminded of the people whose dancing stories have yet to be told.

I must go and see Davy Grady of the Island, near Hospital in Limerick, and there's Joe Ward, one of a rare breed of northern step dancers, who "rattles a step" in a pub on the Carrickmore road out of Omagh. I'm told as well that the traveller McDonagh clan[30] and Felix Doran's daughter have great dancing. Only last week, I managed to track down my old dance teacher, Annie May Fahy, who, at eighty-five, is still as bright as a button and who regaled me with wonderful stories of her life as a teacher and adjudicator, not all of them suitable for publication. I could so easily have missed her. So it goes.

---

30   I am indebted to Martin Maguire of Mell, Drogheda, for this information.

Chapter Six

Social Dance in Ireland

F
AR FROM BEING an isolated, inward-looking community clinging to outdated and quaint manners and customs, Irish society has been part of the wider European cultural scene for many centuries, and all of our group dances have international connections. The modern Irish dance formations derive from both the European mediaeval long-line and couple dances and incorporate elements of both forms. The square dances such as the group jigs and reels, the cotillon and the later quadrilles are related to the old long-line dances and feature the closing of the line into a circle or a "square-for-eight" formation.

The couple style of choral dance finds an echo in the two-hand jig (and latterly reel) which is so distinctively Irish. Here we find the couple dancing hand in hand, separating to dance a "step" and rejoining. Some of these features are also found in the figures of the group jig, reel and quadrille or "set" dances.

Another dance formation found in Ireland is the longways dance in double file with the men and women in straight lines facing each other. This formation is particularly associated with the English country dance or French contradanse. As we have seen, we know from historical accounts that the Irish danced country dances as early as 1600.

Inextricably linked to the dance is its accompanying music. In Ireland since the eighteenth century the most common dance measures have been the reel in 4/4 time or, less commonly, in 2/4 or single reel time; the jig in 6/8, single or double; the 9/8 or hop jig; and the 12/8 jig also known in the south-west of Ireland as the "slide". The hornpipe in 4/4 time is primarily danced solo, though it is often used for the last figure of the set or quadrille-type dance. The polka in 2/4 time is most commonly played for various sets, but is also found as a couple dance in the north of the country.

The dances are here dealt with according to their musical tempo and generally move from the couple dance through three, four, five, six, eight, twelve and sixteen-hand dances to the longways dances "for as many as will".

Jig Dances

Whatever the linguistic origin of the term "jig", commentators are agreed that it refers to the idea of a vigorous up and down movement of the body of which the dance is expressive. In any event, until the early nineteenth century the terms jig, reel and hornpipe have been used interchangeably in Britain and Ireland as formerly none of them was a distinct form in either style or rhythm. The jig has long been associated with Ireland, and the most common form since the eighteenth century at least was the two-hand moneen jig in 6/8 or single jig time with the emphasis on stepping rather than on figures. The name "moneen" from the Irish "móinín", which could be roughly translated as "village green", gave its name to this dance which was, apparently, mainly danced outdoor in the summer months. A detailed description of the dance is given in Crofton Croker's *Legends of the Lakes*.[1] The figures described are as follows:

– Down the middle
– Up again
– Set to your partner
– Change sides
– Set again
– Dance up to your partner

---

1   Thomas Crofton Croker, *Legends of the Lakes*, 2 vols. (London: John Ebers, 1829), p. 185.

- Recede
- Dance up again
- Recede again
- Turn half around with one hand
- Back again with the other
- Set again
- Turn around with both hands
- Bow to the piper.

The commentators on these moneen jigs all express admiration at the skill of the dancers. P.W. Joyce remarks:

> No description can give an idea of the quickness, the dexterity and grace-fulness with which these movements are performed by a variety and minute complication, scarcely a note of music is allowed to pass without its corre-sponding stroke – there are few movements of the human body that require so much skill, dexterity and muscular action all combined.[2]

In common with the solo dance, an interesting feature of these early nineteenth century commentaries is the reference to the male dancer "snapping his fingers" and occasionally "uttering a joyous whoop".[3] The woman danced with arm or arms akimbo. Interestingly, at the same period, a London dancing master was insisting that, for English dancers at least, snapping of fingers and the sudden howl or yell so frequently practised ought particularly to be avoided as partaking too much of the customs of barbarous nations.

An old form of the group jig was known as the "petticoatee". Petrie prints a dance tune called "The Peticoatee Jig" collected from a Clare musician and notes that it accompanied "a species of lively dance once fashionable in Ireland and usually performed immediately after the minuet".[4] This would place the dance as being introduced into Ireland in the late eighteenth–early nineteenth century. An old man in Cavan tells how he learnt the dance from "old people" in 1923. He describes it as "usually

---

2   George Petrie, *Ancient Music of Ireland* (Dublin: 1855), p. 51.
3   Thomas Crofton Croker, *Legends of the Lakes*, p. 194.
4   George Petrie, *Ancient Music of Ireland*, p. 18.

danced by four, no swinging, changing places by hand and introducing a new step after each change". In his area, it was danced to "any double jig tune such as 'The Connachtman's Rambles'".

The jig has also been danced traditionally in four or eight-hand formations in which the couples interact with one another in such movements as chaining; changing place with opposite man or woman; passing through an arch made by one couple; and dancing with joined hands in a circle to left or right. Some four-hand jigs danced traditionally within living memory are "The Siege of Carrick", "The Trip to the Cottage" and, in County Antrim, "Biddy the Basket Woman" and "Hooks and Eyes". These dances and eight-hand jigs such as "The Sweets of May" found their way into publication in *The Irish Folk Dance Books I and II* by Peadar O'Rafferty (1934), *Ár Rincí Foirne* (1939), produced by *An Coimisiún le Rinncí Gaelacha*, and *Dances of Donegal* [5] by Grace Orpen (1931). Some of these dances such as "The Sweets of May" and "The Siege of Carrick" were enthusiastically adopted by the *céilí* dance movement of the Gaelic League and disseminated through the country.

A most unusual four-hand group jig dance known locally as "The Dorricles" has recently come to light in County Cavan.[6] Danced to the popular tune "Haste to the Wedding", it consists of a sequence of figures interspersed with a "body" danced before each figure. There is no break between the figures.

Another category of jig group dance comprises the "sets" or quadrille-type dances. Amongst those using the jig as their main tempo are the Jenny Lind, the castle or Cashel set from Tipperary and the square jig from Kenmare. In Kerry the parts of the set danced to the fast single jig tempo are called slides from a characteristic sliding movement in the steps. Johnny Leary of Gneeveguilla, County Kerry, who has played for dancing since the 1940s, told me that, in his young days, the local sets were composed of four jig figures (double jig tempo); a slide (single jig tempo); and a reel to finish. As he said, "If you played a hornpipe for the last figure, the way it's done now, the dancers would stand looking at you."[7]

---

5   Grace Orpen, *Dances of Donegal* (London: D.M. Wilkie, 1931).
6   A detailed analysis of the choreography of this dance is in progress and will be published in due course.
7   Verbal communication, 1985.

The final group jig dances fall into the category of longways country dances, where a line of men dance opposite a line of women, partner opposite partner. Such dances are "The Waves of Tory", the "Haymaker's Jig", the "Siege of Ennis" and the "Bridge of Athlone". The "Haymaker's Jig" was danced in the tradition prior to its adoption by the Gaelic League in the 1900s and was originally an English longways country dance. As such, it is found in the dance book of a dancing master called Aseh Thompson, who taught the currently fashionable ballroom dances in Dundalk, County Louth, in the late 1800s.[8] "The Waves of Tory" and "The Bridge of Athlone" were possibly newly created by the Gaelic League as being suitable for beginners' classes; they were, in any case, popularised by the League's dance teachers.

The jig in 9/8 time is known as the "hop jig". It is no longer danced traditionally as a group dance. A tantalising glimpse of this lively dance is provided by P.W. Joyce:

> The dance of the hop jig is the most pleasing, airy and graceful of all the Munster dances. It is generally danced by four persons of whom two are females – but the number is not limited. As in the reel, only the alternate parts of the tune are danced; during the other parts the dancers move round the room. In the reel, however, the movement is little more than a mere walk though performed in a systematic way; but in the hop jig the dancers skip lightly round, keeping perfect time with the music – which is played very quickly – and arrive in their respective places in time to commence the "step" to the next part of the tune. The "steps" of the hop jig are quite unlike those of any other dance – they all consist of light and graceful skipping – most exciting, and not at all so fatiguing as the steps of a reel or a double jig. In general the floor is struck or rather tapped lightly, three times during every bar of the tune and from this description the appropriateness of the names "hop jig" and "slip time" will be at once apparent.[9]

---

8   The book is presently owned by Kate Hughes' grandson, Mr F. Maginnis of Wallasey, Cheshire, England. I am indebted to the English dance scholar Joan Flett for facilitating my access to this document.

9   George Petrie, *Ancient Music of Ireland*, p. 62.

Typical hop jig tunes include "The Rocky Road to Dublin" and "Drops of Brandy".

The Reel

Around 1500, a dance including a "hay" or interweaving figure-of-eight or "reeling" movement was imported from France into England and Scotland and thence to Ireland. The English hay-for-three and the Scottish reel-for-three derive from this common origin. In the sixteenth century and seventeenth century, we find references to the "Irish hay" in English popular drama and song.

The musical connection between this early hay or reel form and the modern reel in 4/4 time with its characteristic bars of

is not discernible, as the printed music collections contain no Irish hay. Indeed it is not until the late eighteenth century that identifiably Irish reels appear in print, although Scottish reels such as "Miss McLeod's", "Lord McDonnell" and "Rakish Paddy" were, and still are, universally popular in Ireland.

The two-hand reel was an adaptation of the older jig form but it differed in some respects. The reel was much less fatiguing in that the dance involved 8 bars of stepping, alternating with 8 bars of promenading around the room, this alternation continuing usually to the end of the dance. The jig, however, required almost continuous dancing with only occasional movement around the floor for relaxation. Again, as in the jig, the earlier steps were lighter, whereas later, more demanding and fatiguing steps were done.

A dance which contained a reeling figure was notated in Wexford in the early 1800s. The accompanying music was, however, not a reel but somewhat akin to a jig, only slower. A version of the actual reel-for-three as danced in County Cavan in the late 1800s was notated in 1956. Interestingly, the oldest layer of this dance seems to involve three male dancers. As the informant says:

There was a real old way of doing the three-hand-reel. I often saw three fellows dancing it. The three would lead round first. They danced the old traditional steps all the time – there wasn't a note of the music but they hit. You'd think their feet were drumsticks. After they led around the boy in the centre turned to his right and danced with the boy on his right, while the boy on the left remained idle. The boy in the centre turned and danced with the boy on the left and the boy on the right remained idle. Then they danced round in a circle and, after that, they chained. Then the boy that was in the centre at first went to the right and the boy that was at the right went into the centre. Before they made that change they danced in and out through each other [this is the figure-of-eight movement associated with the reel group dance] and danced into their new positions. Then, the boy in the centre danced with the fellow on his right and turned and danced with the fellow on his left. They danced around in a circle again, chained again and danced through each other into new positions, the fellow that was last in the centre going to the left and the fellow on the left going to the centre. They danced the same way as before and then the three of them faced the onlookers and finished up the reel with the best steps they could think of.[10]

A detailed description of an old four-hand reel is given by Patrick Kennedy. The directions are quite clear and include such elements as "circle left and right", "hands across", "chaining" and "setting" (dancing in place), which occur so frequently in the Irish group dance tradition.

Two young men and their partners stood in a circle holding hands and at the conclusion of Shamus's [the musician's] prelude footed it around till they were in their original places. At the first bar of the second part, away they went again in an opposite direction. Then the men, joining their right hands in the centre and the women imitating them, another revolution was made, followed by one contrariwise, the left hands being connected. The next move was a change of places between the men and a return to the old ground accompanied by a corresponding movement on the part of the women. This cross-fire had a very good effect when neatly executed. They then passed round giving right hand to first person met, left hand to second

10   James Argue, Copponagh, Co. Cavan, 1951, Irish Folklore Commission, vol. 1209, pp. 597–8.

etc. till after describing two circles, they arrived at home again. Each man now facing his partner, went through the regular advances, retreats, "variates", side-steps, sets to etc. till the "hooking" impulse set them at work in this direction. They varied this exercise by the men taking right hands in the middle and changing places and then giving left hand and recovering their own ground. They then looked on while the women executed a similar manoeuvre. The finale was the taking of hands and bowing or curtseying to opposite partners and then the forming of a line and saluting the dancing-master.[11]

The detail in this description gives us an invaluable picture of the group dance tradition in the pre-quadrille period in Ireland. The quadrilles had not at this stage (1813) been performed even in the fashionable salons of London and Dublin, much less in rural Ireland. The "pleasing evolutions" of the dancers observed by Kennedy owe nothing to the formulations of the quadrilles since they obviously predate them. So much for the claims of many leading nationalist figures in the early 1900s that the four-hand reel was the illegitimate child of the quadrilles and thus unsuitable for Irish dancing feet. Many other examples of four-hand reels are described or adverted to by O'Keefe and O'Brien and by J.J. Sheehan,[12] providing evidence of the widespread popularity of this dance form as well as its variety.

The leading Kerry dancing master, Tadhg Sheáin Uí Shúilleabháin gave O'Keefe and O'Brien a reel dance called "*Fionn-ala*" which mainly involved side steps and chaining figures; Professor Reidy of Kerry contributed a four-hand "square reel", called after a figure in the dance which involved each of the four dancers side stepping in the pattern of a square. An unusual four-hand reel from Donegal "sometimes called the Scottish reel" is referred to, in which the

> . . . men stand back to back and the women face their partners. During the first half of the tune, the dancers perform a figure resembling the figure-of-eight, the men falling in with opposite partners alternately and the women always returning to their own place. They dance a step to the second half of

---

11   Patrick Kennedy, "Irish Dancing Fifty Years Ago", *Dublin University Magazine*, vol. LXII (1863), p. 435.

12   J.J. Sheehan, A *Guide to Irish Dancing* (Dublin & New York: John Denvir, 1902).

the tune and start off again at the turn of the music. This is a graceful and lively reel.[13]

Whilst the detail here is somewhat rudimentary, the evidence of a reeling or figure-of-eight movement is quite clear. This "Scotch" or "Scottish" reel has been notated mainly in northern counties, which may be explained by the historical movement of migrant labourers from this region to and from Scotland.

An unusual and entertaining formation – the five-hand reel – has been noted in various locations. In one Donegal version it is known as the *stocaire* – the "intruder" or odd-man out. The dance is a form of game in which a man or woman is excluded by the other four participants and the music is stopped in order to allow the excluded dancer to attempt to re-enter the group. A Connemara version of this dance is known as *an stocaire* or, more commonly, as *an robairín*.[14] Here, a cloth or handkerchief is used. The cloth is passed among the dancers from man to woman and the man who finally ends up holding it has to stand in the middle of the circle until he is replaced by the next victim. A Donegal version notated by Grace Orpen in 1931 is there known as the pin dance. A version from County Cavan was taken down in 1951 from a man of ninety who saw it danced in his young days. "One boy or girl would rest during one part of the dance; then, they'd join in and someone else would take their place."[15]

The six-hand reel was often danced by four women (x) and two men (o), commencing thus:

```
      X     X
      O     O
      X     X
```

The basic format was: advance, retire, "ringing" in two circles to right and left, a figure involving side stepping, elbow chain and a final side step figure – to be repeated at the discretion of the dancers. This version of the six-hand Fairy Reel can be found in O'Keefe and O'Brien's dance handbook. It was collected in Marblehill, County Donegal. Indeed, most printed

---

13   J.G. O'Keefe and Art O'Brien, A *Handbook of Irish Dances* (Dublin: O'Donoghue & Co., 1902), p. 117.
14   *Robairín* – dishcloth, a cloth for drying dishes, from the English "rubber".
15   James Argue, I.F.C., vol. 1209, p. 602.

versions of the six-hand reel have been collected in northern counties. Another six-hand reel – the Duke reel – can be found in Orpen's *Dances of Donegal*. This dance has been documented in the living tradition in County Fermanagh. Mick Hoy, the fiddler from Derrygonnelly in Fermanagh, explains the title thus: "Ye have to *jook* in and out under other's *oxters* [armpits]. That's how it got the name!"[16]

The eight-hand reel was very widespread in the tradition until the late nineteenth century when the quadrilles became the popular eight-hand reel dance. A singular aspect of eight-hand reel dancing was the custom of paying the musician at the conclusion of each eight-hand reel. P.W. Joyce describes it thus:

> It is an object with the musician to procure the recurrence of the eight-hand reel as frequently as possible; for the men who dance it always pay him. On first standing out after the eight-hand reel – which passes off without any immediate payment, this being reserved for the dance succeeding – each man puts a piece of money into the hands of his partner, who hands it to the musician. This payment varies from a penny up to a shilling, but seldom goes above two pence; as the same person may have to pay several times during the same evening. The payment, however, of a shilling, or any large sum in the commencement exempts the person from further charge. Among the poorer class of peasantry, each man pays one penny – seldom more – every time he dances a reel. The woman frequently increases the offering by an addition of her own; but this is an act of generosity from which, if she please, she may always exempt herself.[17]

The reel set or quadrille-style dances achieved widespread popularity in the late nineteenth century and early twentieth century. Sets such as the Orange and Green and the Caledonian achieved great popularity in the south-west of the country, with the Caledonian set surviving in Clare into modern times. Older dancers such as Dan Furey in Labasheeda, County Clare, remember the Paris set which was danced locally.

An interesting feature in the recent development of sets is that occasionally a set such as the Baile Bhúirne reel set retains that name,

---

16   Mick Hoey, Derrygonnelly, County Fermanagh. 1985, coll. Seán Corcoran.
17   George Petrie, *Ancient Music of Ireland*, p. 60.

although the set is now danced to polkas. The popularity of the "polka" tempo, which is actually the older single reel (2/4), is noticeable in the south of the country. In Counties Tipperary, Waterford, Kerry and Cork, the polka rhythm now dominates the sets.

Group reel dances for over four couples are rare in the tradition. A dance programme of the Lambeg Irish Folk Dance Society for 10 January 1934 includes a performance of a twelve-hand reel "as danced in the Castlewellan district of County Down". It was danced to the "Teetotaller's Reel".

The largest group reel is a sixteen-hand dance which was, as we have already seen, confined to open-air dances at crossroads or other such locations. A sixteen-hand reel is still danced traditionally on Tory Island, off the coast of Donegal. I have taken down two versions of the sixteen-hand reel from the Louth/Meath area where they were known as the "set" and were danced at outdoor gatherings at, amongst other places, Beaulieu Cross near Baltray and at the gates of Gormanstown Castle.

Couple Dances

Apart from the couple jig and reel dances which were universally popular in Ireland, there exists a large body of dance for individual couples performing movements on their own quite independent of other dancers. Of these couple dances most, if not all, originate in the fashionable ballroom dances of the nineteenth century and are usually known as "circle" or "round" dances from the idea that the dancing couples circle the floor in a clockwise direction. They were introduced into the ballroom repertoire at various times during the century: the waltz in 1816, the polka in 1844, the scottische in 1850 and the varsovienne in 1853. These dances and their offshoots moved from the ballrooms of "polite society", often via the dancing masters, to the countryside where they were adapted to the native dance steps and music.

Many of these dances involve the couple commencing side by side, moving forward for 4 bars (7 "steps"), turning, moving back to place (4 bars); repeating all foregoing; then in a "waltz hold" dancing around for 16 bars – the whole sequence commencing again and so on until the music stops.

The varsovienne, often called in Ireland the "verse" or even in one instance the "verse of piano", was universally popular and is often known by the name of the dance song which was sung to accompany the dance. For instance, it is most commonly known as "Shoe the Donkey" from the verse; "Shoe the donkey, shoe the donkey, shoe the donkey's right toe." I collected a version in Louth which included directions for the dance and is known there as "Judy Elcock". "Judy Elcock, Judy Elcock, put your right foot down here", etc. It also turns up in Cork as "Father Halpin" from the verse "Father Halpin, Father Halpin, Father Halpin's top coat"; and even – having moved far from its polite ballroom origins – "Cock your leg up, cock your leg up, cock your leg up, said she."

The scottische began its life as a European ballroom couple dance incorporating what were considered as Scottish style steps and rapidly became universally popular all over the Continent producing many variations. It was danced traditionally in every part of Ireland under various names. In the north it is generally called the Highland, in Clare and Cavan it was known as the fling, in Cork as the Highland fling and in other areas some variant of "seteesh" or "satoosh". In some areas it is danced to a particular tune and is known by this name. In south Connemara they use "Johnny/Love, won't you marry me?" and is there known simply as "The Johnny". In the Connemara area of Renvyle, it is known as "The Tommio". In Mayo and Roscommon it is known as "The Keel Row" from the tune of the same name.

The Highland is widespread in Ireland, and I have collected many variants of it, including, in Donegal, the Highland *garbhríocha* (rough Highland) in which the stepping is more emphatic and the leg movements wilder and more flamboyant than the standard version. The term *garbh* is used by the dancers themselves, though it probably originally derives from an outsider's view of the dance.

Although this section is concerned with couple dances, it feels appropriate to include here mention of the Irish Highland, which is a dance for three – two women and a man, who is located between the two women, holding each by the nearest hand. All three dance forward together, dance backwards back to place (twice), and then the women move in turn under the man's arms in a series of fluid "juking" patterns. I have collected versions of this dance in Sligo and Fermanagh but have not seen or heard of it in any county further south. In some parts of the country, particularly in the north, there exists a large repertoire of tunes for the scottische or Highland. A northern player will sometimes "Highland" a reel, giving it what is known locally as a "snap": in other words adapting it to the distinctive staccato "Scottish style" rhythm of this dance.

Also widespread is the Stack of Barley or Seven Steps, with its variant the Stack of Wheat. These dances by and large involve a side step to the left, then to the right (8 bars); repeating the foregoing (8 bars); then, finally, a dance around (16 bars). This pattern is repeated till the music stops. It is not possible to give a definitive version of this dance as regional variations abound.

The polka is also popular as a dance rhythm, though its use as a tempo for couple dances appears more widespread in the north of the country where it appears as a "Kick polka" in Fermanagh and a "Berlin polky" in Donegal.

The waltz is universally known and is usually called simply the "old time". The valeta – another waltz-type dance – achieved widespread popularity during this century, as did its ballroom companion the military two-step, which was often danced to Irish marches such as "O'Donnell Abú". The barndance (based on the older "pas de quatre"), which originated in America in the 1880s, became hugely popular in Ireland and developed many variants. Occasionally it was danced to a particular tune, as in Monaghan where it became "Kitty Got her Blinking".

Various other simple couple dances, such as the Cuckoo's Nest, the German or German scottische, the Marine and the Corn Rigs (corny rakes), were popular for brief periods in the twentieth century, particularly in the north of the country. The most popular surviving couple dances in the tradition are the various versions of the varsovienne and the scottische, the Stack of Barley and the ubiquitous waltz.

Generally speaking, the main corpus of Irish group dance can be seen to conform to patterns found widespread in Europe. The distinctive Irish flavour accorded to all these forms derives from the accompanying dance rhythms of the reel, jig, polka, slide and hornpipe as played in Ireland, as well as the characteristic stepping patterns of the traditional dance style.

IRISH DANCE

To J.J. Sheehan, an Irish dancing master of the late nineteenth century, we give the last word on the subject of Irish group dance. What it lacks in scientific objectivity it more than makes up for in patriotic fervour:

Let foreigners brag and crow
That dancing's their devotion
'Tis little the craychurs know
Of the poetry of motion;
Their polkas and quadrilles
Are nothin' else but prancin'
An' Irish jigs and reels
The King and Queen of dancin'.

Chapter Seven

Gambles, Prinkums and Biddy Balls:
Traditional Dance Occasions

I N THE TWENTIETH century, the world of dance in Ireland changed almost beyond recognition in little more than a generation. To the young people of the 1950s and 1960s, the terms "swarees" (soireés), "rips", "prinkums", "tournaments" and "kitchen rackets" had become unrecognisable as the names for nights of dance fun. Yet the memory of these occasions remained vivid amongst the men and women of the previous generation who had themselves organised their own amusement, and the current dominance of the hotel and lounge bar in the celebration of important life events was simply unknown. The key to the disappearance of so many features of cultural life in Ireland in this century lies in a complex of social change brought about by factors such as emigration, migration from rural to urban centres of population, with their consequent social dislocation, but a hugely influential event was, undoubtedly, the passing of a piece of legislation known as the Public Dance Hall Act (1935). This law had the effect, whether intentionally or not, of effectively killing the house dances which had formerly been an indispensable part of life in rural Ireland.

The names used for different dance occasions varied from one area to another. The term "ball" to describe a dance occasion was in common usage but it could represent many quite different types of social event. A ball often had overtones of a more upper-class affair, akin to a modern dress dance. It was an invitation-only gathering and was often organised by the clergy in the local school house. "Ba ócáidí galánta iad seo. 'Daoine móra' is mó a bhí ann."[1] ("These were fancy occasions, mainly attended by 'important people'.")

In Meath, we are told: "Very early in my memory [c.1904], there used to be a ball in the school now and then. I imagine it was the better-off people that went to it. At school the next day we used to have a feast on the remains of the supper – meat and bread and cakes and the master used to make tea for us all with it."[2]

In some areas, a ball could simply mean an ordinary house dance, whereas in others, it was used to indicate a type of gathering which would be unacceptable to polite society, as in the Biddy Balls which followed a day of celebration of the folk custom of carrying a decorated doll known as a Brídeog through the countryside on St Brigid's eve (31 January). Groups of "biddies" went from house to house, where in return for a small subscription they sang, played music and danced a "bout" of dance. They then pooled their collections, and having obtained the use of some farmer's house, they set about arranging a "great night". Tea, sugar, bread and butter and of course a good supply of porter were provided, and with the help of the farmer's family a great session of dancing went on all night and often until late on the following day. These dances, dubbed "porter balls" by a disapproving clergy, were seen by the Catholic Church as having unacceptably pagan overtones and were often denounced from the pulpit by the clergy of the area.

The word "spree" indicated a dance held in a local house – more a party. The following account, from Mrs Margaret Conway, the noted folklorist from Ballivor, County Meath, gives a wonderfully evocative picture of such a night's fun:

---

1   Séamus Ó Tónra, An Cheathrú Rua, Co. na Gaillimhe, 1969, Irish Folklore Commission dance questionnaire.
2   Mrs Margaret Conway, Ballivor, Co. Meath, 1969, I.F.C. dance questionnaire.

There might be a "spree" in a house where someone was going to America, or home from America or England for a holiday. At a "spree", the immediate neighbours would be sure to be invited, also relatives and the friends of different members of the family, boys and girls, but there might be as many elderly people as young people. There would be a little whiskey and wine but the main drink would be porter – a half-barrel or a quarter cask, according to means and numbers and a case of lemonade for the girls and children. Only the old men and women, I think, would have the wine and whiskey. There would be no one drunk. There would be tea also during the night, in the kitchen. The dancing might, in small houses, be in the kitchen too but if they had a big room, it was cleared out for it or the barn, and boards were put on blocks or stools around the walls for seats.

The actual dances were chiefly sets (quadrilles) or more usually half-sets except there was a lot of room and a big crowd. Now and then there was a set of Lancers and now and then some of the men did a step dance – jig, reel or hornpipe – and I remember some of the old people – a man and two women – doing a three-hand reel. I remember a man who lived near us who had worked for some time in the "North" (south Armagh, I think) and he always did a special dance across a long straw on the floor. The was also a dance called by us a "Seteesh" [scottische]. Also, the Waltz was coming in and one or two could do it and the Military Two-Step (for which they always played the "Soldier's Chorus" from "Faust"). There were always songs between dances at any dance.[3]

Mrs Conway has some interesting observations to make concerning the repertoire of songs which were popular in the period, and her comments on the performers' choice of song are quite illuminating:

The more "backward" sang things like "If I was a Blackbird" or "Bound for Charlestown." Better-up people sang the "Swanee River" type or the music-hall comics and Scottish songs such as "Annie Laurie" were great favourites. The old patriotic-ballad singers' songs like "Bould Robert Emmet" were perhaps sung by old men but the young fellows thought them old-fashioned. The musical people with ambitions – or an opinion of

---

3   Ibid.

themselves, sang "Killarney" and an odd one even had "The Lost Chord" or "Rocked in the Cradle of the Deep". When the Gaelic League came [c.1917], the favourites were Brian O'Higgins', chiefly "Moses Ri-tooril". Sometimes, someone gave a recitation – one man always did "Fontenoy".[4]

As part of the night's fun, there might be a dance such as the "shoe dance", which was a kind of ice-breaker. This dance from Cavan went as follows: "All the girls took off one shoe and threw them in a heap in the centre of the floor. The fellows then rushed to the heap, and every fellow that could get hold of a shoe picked it up and went round looking for the owner. And when he found the owner, she had to dance with him."[5] At the old house dances in Louth, I was told by Harry Fairtclough of Drogheda, the night's fun finished with a dance where a woman sat on a chair in the middle of the floor and every man had to kiss every woman in the house. The woman sitting on the chair escaped the kiss.

In general, at house dances, singing and solo dancing featured either in between group dances or for the last hour or two of the night. Then an exhibition of step dancing would begin and occasionally a spirit of friendly rivalry would take over with dancers "facing each other" and trying to "tire each other down".

Some dances were essentially impromptu and indeed, in areas such as west Clare, such was the passion for dancing that occasionally, when a group of men found themselves in a house of an evening with no available female partners, they would organise a "buck set" or a "buck lancer", in other words a male-only formation. James Keane of Labasheeda told me that he even danced with a tongs for a partner if one man of the eight was missing, and the tongs was ceremoniously passed from man to man in the fifth figure of the Caledonian, in place of the more usual human partner! A broom or brush was often used in the same way, hence the oft-heard remark of the city-slicker about the supposed dullness of rural life: "Sure, you haven't lived until you've done the Pass the Brush dance!"

From near Athlone in the County Westmeath comes an account of a "kitchen racket" which was an informal dance held in a farmhouse:

---

4   I*bid.*
5   James Argue, (90) Copponagh, Co. Cavan, 1951, coll. P.J. Gaynor, I.F.C., vol. 1209, p. 601.

Those dances were held in the winter-time. They had in a particular house what was called the "joined melodeon". In other words, each village collected the money perhaps over a long period of time as money was scarce in those days and then bought the melodeon. The young people met inside or outside this house any night they felt like a dance. They got the "music box" as it was sometimes called. They then struck up a tune; all marched after the music and they bowled into the first house that they crossed and danced their shoes off till the late hours of the morning.[6]

Another type of impromptu dance was known in Cavan as a "surprise party":

A couple of fellows would get together and have a chat about it, and they'd make what you'd call the preliminary arrangements. They'd decide to have the party in such a house on such a night, and the people of the house would know nothing about it at all. A good number of fellows in the locality would be called together and told about it and each man was served out with a slip of paper. On that paper was written the goods that he was to bring to the party . . . It was a funny business and they'd have a good night. There would be no porter unless they "joined" and paid so much apiece for it.[7]

A popular type of house dance combined with card-playing was known as a "tournament" and was held on winter nights, particularly coming up to Christmas. Geese, turkeys, and homemade knitwear and basketwork were played for, and those who were not interested in cards came to dance. The card-playing was held in one room of the house, the dancing in another. Local musicians provided the music. If the house was very crowded, the musician's chair was put up on the table so that he could play without fearing for his instrument.

Another category of dance which was a feature of rural life was the so-called "joined dance" where the poorer people joined forces and subscribed towards the cost of food and drink. "This would be frowned upon – not respectable – and the priests would be against it." The term prinkum (from the Irish *princeam* – gambolling or frolicking) was used in many areas

---

6   Thomas Kelly, Curraghboy, Athlone, Co. Westmeath, 1969, I.F.C. dance questionnaire.
7   Michael Carroll (75), Bailieboro, Co. Cavan, 1951, I.F.C., vol. 1209, pp. 550–1.

in the west of Ireland to denote a joined dance. An account from County Galway tells us:

> The word was in pretty frequent use in my own young days [c.1900] and is still used by older people. The older people referred to the little country house balls – a subscription dance where drink was supplied – as a prinkum. Sometimes a raffle was held in connection with this dance with a clock, a watch, or a goat as the prize. Sometimes a quite respectable dance given by a person to friends and relations would be referred to enviously by a person not invited as a prinkum. This does not imply that the prinkum was a low affair but as not reaching the standards of respectability of an invitation dance.[8]

The mention of a raffle as part of a prinkum in Galway has echoes in the use of the term "raffle" to indicate a dance which was arranged by a family which had fallen on hard times to gather funds to, for instance, help them pay their rent. A dancer from Fermanagh told me that neighbours would whitewash the inside of the house prior to such a dance and that occasionally the white marks on a guest's clothing would later betray his attendance at the raffle, which would be frowned on by the socially pretentious families in the area.[9]

In Gaelic-speaking Rann na Feirste, in Donegal, the English word was used for the event. "If you got a new pair of shoes and they didn't fit, you'd get up a 'raffle' for them. If they didn't fit the man who won them, he'd have a 'raffle', and so on!"[10] During the Second World War 'raffles' for bicycle lamps or cigarettes made a tidy sum for their musician organisers.

A marvellous insight into the social attitudes inherent in the class structure of rural Ireland in the early twentieth century and the way that dance occasions and dance repertoire reflected these is contained in an account by Patrick Finn of Loughrea, County Galway. Though much of the account is somewhat humorously phrased, it still conveys the deep social divisions of the period. He tells us:

---

8   Padraig Discin, Milltown, Co. Galway, 1941, I.FC., vol. 1144, p. 21.
9   Vincent Duffy, Garrison, Co. Fermanagh, 1985. Verbal communication.
10 John Gráinne Devenny, interview with Seán Corcoran, SCDAT 14, ITMA, 1995. Translated from Irish.

My first dance was at a wedding in 1909. It was in a big barn with a good concrete floor and two oil lamps gave light. There was one melodeon and three men and a girl played it in turn. The rule seemed to be a different dance after the last one. They danced Quadrilles or as it was called, the Plain set and the Reel set. The Lancers, which seemed to require more skill, was danced once or twice. After each set, a polka was danced and partners were changed. Then a Fling, danced in pairs, the Military two-step, sets again and then the Valeta waltz. There was no M.C. [Master of Ceremonies]. The music seemed to regulate what the next dance would be. When there was a lull, somebody called for a song. One man sang "A Nation Once Again", another sang about someone who shaved with a gapped razor.

Dances were mostly held in farm-kitchens. Sometimes the manager [the parish priest] gave the local school for a concert followed by a dance but this was very rare. There was a long narrow room at the top of a high house in Loughrea. The elite, a couple of times a year, held a "ball" there, never a "dance". The top "ball" was the R.I.C. one. Waltz, Polka, and Lancers were the thing. Reel sets were for the lesser breeds, without the law. In every locality, in winter, there was an organised dance in a big barn. The men paid 2/-, the girls were free. There was usually a half-barrel of stout (never in bottles), a case of lemonade and tea. Sometimes, the young bloods from the town or the sons of country shopkeepers would patronise these "swarees". Their fathers were probably gombeen men, but the sons looked on those affairs as good fun but not to be taken seriously and they could not possibly master the tribal dances.[11]

The barn was a universally popular location for a dance and the loft, which had a wooden floor, was an ideal spot. Dances in barns were often held at the end of a harvest when the farmer and his family would hold a dance for the *meitheal* or team of neighbours who had combined to bring in the crop. In areas where flax was a major crop, particularly in the northern counties of Antrim, Tyrone, etc., flax-scutching or lint-pulling dances were organised by the farm owner. An account from Antrim tells us:

---

11   Patrick Finn, Boher Dhu, Loughrea, Co. Galway, 1969, I.F.C. dance questionnaire.

Wooden floors in barns acquired a polish from the straw and sacks stored there, which made them ideal for dancing. In addition, a wooden floor lent itself to impromptu percussion from the farm boots of the dancers. At the flax-pulling time the barn would be nearly empty so there would be plenty of room for dancing. The choice of the dances is often left to the girls; but before they have made up their minds the fiddler starts another eight-hand reel. There is a certain humour in this, because the custom required the musician to be paid after every eight-hand reel, so naturally it is his favourite dance.[12]

The following account of barn dances from Baronscourt, County Tyrone, gives some fascinating detail about the type of dances which were locally popular at the turn of the twentieth century, as well as providing a gently humorous view of the "stricter Presbyterian" attitude to dancing:

It was the custom at Baronscourt to have two annual dances in the barn to celebrate "Harvest Home" and Christmas, and to these dances my father, and my brother after him, invited every single person in their employ, and all the neighbouring farmers and their wives. Anyone hoping to shine at a barn dance required exceptionally sound muscles, for the dancing was quite a serious business. The so-called barn was really a long granary, elaborately decorated with wreaths of evergreen, flags and mottoes. The proceedings invariably commenced with a dance (peculiar I think to the north of Ireland) known as "Haste to the Wedding". It is a country dance, but its peculiarity lies in the fact that, instead of the couples standing motionless opposite to one another, they are expected to "set to each other" and to keep on doing steps without intermission; all this being, I imagine, typical of the intense eager-ness every one was supposed to express to reach the scene of the wedding festivities as quickly as possible. Twenty minutes of "Haste to the Wedding" are warranted to exhaust the stoutest leg muscles. My mother always led off with the farm bailiff as partner, my father at the other end dancing with the bailiff's wife. Both my father and my brother after him were very careful to wear their Garter as well as their other Orders on these occasions, in order to show respect to their guests. Scotch reels and Irish jigs alternated with

---

12   Cahal Dallet,"The Lint-pulling Dance", *Journal of the Glens of Antrim Historical Society*, vol. 6 (1978), p. 11.

the "Triumph", "Flowers of Edinburgh" and other country dances, until feet and legs refused their office, and still the fiddles scraped and feet, light or heavy, belaboured the floor till 6 a.m. The supper would hardly have come up to London standards, for instead of light airy nothings, huge joints of roast and boiled meat were laid down the tables. Some of the stricter Presbyterians, though fond of a dance, expressed conscientious qualms about it. So they struck an ingenious compromise with their consciences by dancing vigorously whilst assuming an air of intense misery, as though they were undergoing some terrible penance. Everyone present enjoyed these barn dances enormously.[13]

Unlike the barn, many country houses had a clay floor where a dancer "could not get his tips", that is, could not make the sharp tapping sounds so characteristic of Irish step dance. In this situation, it was common to use the door of the house as a surface for dancers, particularly for solo performance. There would be a shout: "Take down the door!" The door would be taken off the "buckans" (*bacáin*) and put on the floor. A dancer from Leitrim remembers how, in the days before electric light, extra candles would be lit and two fellows, each with a candle, would go down on one knee holding the light so that everyone could see his dancing.

Some solid, well-built farmhouses had flag-stone floors. These hard surfaces were ideal for dancing. It was customary to put sometimes a horse's skull, sometimes an iron cooking pot under the large flag nearest the fire. These acted as resonators, and an opportunity to dance on this spot was highly prized. When, in the course of a dance, a couple landed on this flag, it was an opportunity for the man to demonstrate his skill in battering out the rhythm of the music. Occasionally, it seems, competition for this favoured dancing spot could become fierce. A penny or twopence got one the flag for a certain space of time. The dancers had the option of throwing another penny or two into the musician's hat and holding the flag for a continuous dancing period. There used to be considerable rivalry as to who would hold the flag the longest among different factions in the locality.

---

13   Lord Frederic Hamilton, *The Days Before Yesterday*, 26th ed. (London: Hodder and Stoughton, 1937), pp. 304–5. First published 1920.

Near Derrygonnelly in County Fermanagh a flag was used to provide a firm footing over a small stream which ran under a byroad. Dancers loved this flag as it provided an ideal surface for the dancer to rattle a step or two. One night, a devotee of the Terpsichorean art landed on the flag, tapped out a step and, "Declare to God, the poor man couldn't stop dancing, no matter what he did. It was a fairy flag, you see. When he was found in the morning, he wasn't able to wag."[14]

The account of paying a musician to gain a dance advantage leads us to the topic of dance occasions which were directly organised by musicians. In Mayo, these were organised mainly by fiddlers, as it happens. Called "school dances", they were actually held in country houses and were unconnected with schooling in any form.[15] The usage of this term does not appear in any account outside Mayo. The nearest equivalent comes from County Longford, where a fiddler would organise a "week's dance" in a local barn. The primary focus of the County Mayo school dances was that apart from providing entertainment for the local young people, they were a source of livelihood for the musicians. They were held during the winter months (from November to February) and each school dance lasted for up to two weeks.

The following account gives a very comprehensive picture of this custom:

In regards to the old traditional dances that used to be held in my district in the country houses, they used to be called the "School Dances". These dances would be started on a Sunday night by two musicians. They would be two fiddlers or a fiddle-player and a melodeon player or perhaps a fiddle and flute-player. So, the dance would be carried on for two weeks every night during that time. There might be four villages in the district included in the school-dance. They would hold the dances in different houses during the fortnight, maybe two nights in some houses. So at the end of the fortnight, it would be on a Sunday night, all the boys and girls who would be attending the dance during that time would pay 1/- each or perhaps some would pay 2/- each to the musicians. At the beginning of the school-dance, all the names of the boys and girls who would attend the dance would be taken.

14   Jimmy Maguire, Derrygonnelly, Co. Fermanagh, 1985, coll. Seán Corcoran.
15   The term may be an echo of earlier dancing-school practice. As used here, it does not imply any form of tuition.

Two views of Irish dancing, Martin Place, Sydney, September 1976 (National Library of Australia)

Sydney Irish Ceili Dancers at the Pride of Erin Festival, Yass, NSW, March 1996

Young dancers from the Canberra Irish Club at the Pride of Erin Festival, Yass, NSW, 1996. Musicians are Marcolm Bilton & Bridget Allen.

Set Dancing at Gleesons of Coore, Miltown Malbay, Co. Clare 1999 (Tony Kearns)

An Irish jig, Killarney (Irish Traditional Music Archive)

Dancing competition, Pléaráca Chonamara, Connemara 1

Dancing competition, Pléaráca Chonamara, Connemara 2

Dancing competition, Pléaráca Chonamara, Connemara 3

Dancing competition, Pléaráca Chonamara, Connemara 4

Dancing competition, Pléaráca Chonamara, Connemara 5

Barry John Gallagher, World Irish Dancing championships, Limerick 1991 (The Irish Times)

Richie Reece, World Irish Dancing championships, Dublin April 1994 (Matt Kavanagh, The Irish Times)

There might be about 70 or 80 boys and girls. All those names would be called out on the night the school-dance would finish. That would be the pay-night and the musicians would get £4 or £5 at the end of the fortnight. I often played the fiddle myself at those dances. We would start the dance at 7 o'clock and continue until midnight every night during the fortnight that is, during the winter months. The "school-dances" would begin on the 1st of November and continue on until the 1st February.

The speaker, John Bartley, concludes by saying: "But as you know, all those local dances in the country-houses are banned since the Dance Halls came into existence."[16] This must have had a devastating effect on the livelihood of many musicians.

A series of dances organised by a musician was known in Longford as a "week's dance":

A fiddler in the district would give out that he was going to have a week's dance in some barn in the district. Every one would turn up every night for the dance. The dance would start about eight or nine in the evening and would be over at twelve or one o' clock usually. The dancing would go on for the whole week and the last dance of the week would be held of a Sunday night. The fiddler would then make a collection and all the men paid three-pence. The women paid nothing. The dances were jigs, reels and set-dances.[17]

The custom of musicians organising dances for a living was a survival of an older period when it was commonplace for musicians to be sup-ported by a community. For instance, in the home place of Captain O'Neill, Tralibane in County Kerry, "The parish supported two professional pipers in the years after the Famine: Charley Murphy, or *Cormac na bPaidreacha*, who had a regular outdoor pitch at Tralibane Bridge, a few hundred yards from the O'Neill home, and Peter Hagerty, An *Píobaire Bán*, who played at the nearby Colomane crossroads."[18]

---

16 John Bartley, Pollatomish, Ballina, Co. Mayo, 1969, I.F.C. dance questionnaire.
17 Patrick Hetherton (75), Aughnacliffe, parish of Columkille, Co. Longford, 1955, coll. Jim Delaney, I.F.C., vol. 1430, p. 148.
18 Nicholas Carolan, A *Harvest Saved* (Cork: Ossian Publications, 1997), p. 7.

By the twentieth century, this type of dance occasion, organised by a musician, was a relative rarity. Most dances were free of charge. From Longford comes a poignant account of the changes which had been wrought in the social life of the area since the passing of the Dance Hall Act. The collector reports that:

> All the old people are at one in condemning the commercial dances, now so common in every parish. Most of them are outraged at the idea of having to pay three or four shillings for a night's dance, when in their day, the dances were absolutely free. There is a general distrust and dislike by the old people of these dance-halls, which they think are menacing the older and better and more sociable way of life of their young days.[19]

Apart from the financial repercussions to musicians, the main result of the forced relocation of dance nights from the houses of rural Ireland to the commercial halls during the late 1930s and '40s was the loss of control by the people of various social occasions in which dance was central. The suppression of the house dances, together with the growth of an entrepreneurial culture which saw the opportunity to develop the Irish passion for dancing into a profitable industry, led inexorably to the construction of the gigantic and highly lucrative "ballrooms of romance" which became a feature of the landscape of rural Ireland in the 1950s and '60s.

Some dance occasions continued to be home based, however. Amongst these was the so-called "American (or Australian) wake" which was held on the eve of the emigration of a family member. Known, chillingly, as a "live wake" in some areas, it signalled the perception of the period that the emigré was, to all intents and purposes, soon to be lost to the living. It is only in relatively recent times that emigrants could return easily to visit their families in Ireland, and the devastating effect of the loss of a beloved son or daughter was marked by a social event which mirrored the rites of passage surrounding physical death. An account of such an event from Cavan tells us:

> When people would be going to America for the first time, there was nearly always a dance held in their parents' house and their own people and

---

19   John Murtagh, (77), Clonelly, Dromard, Co. Longford, 1955, I.F.C., vol. 1429, p. 150.

friends and neighbours would be there. Everyone that came to it would be welcome. It was a lonesome sort of dance because the son or daughter of the house was leaving to go so far away and wouldn't come home again for many a long year. And in many cases they were leaving, never to return, although they didn't think that at the time. You might say it was a dance with a gloom over it. The members of the family that were remaining at home would be the saddest of them all. I was at several dances of this kind and you couldn't enjoy them very much. Any enjoyment that was at them wasn't a natural enjoyment. There was always a cloud hanging over a dance like that.[20]

In some areas, it was customary to sing only sad songs at such a dance, which added to the gloomy atmosphere. The wake lasted all night and the dawn was the signal for the dreaded moment of parting. Friends and neighbours would escort the emigrant to the port of departure, but the mother remained at home to privately mourn the loss of her child.

In the north of Ireland, the farewell dance was known as a convoy. The accomplished fiddler and dancer Charlie O'Neill, now living in the Moy in County Tyrone, grew up in the Blue Stacks region of south Donegal. He gives us an idea of the devastating effect of emigration on his home area when he says that in the 1920s, "400 left Donegal town one Monday, a lot of them from my district".[21] The return of emigrants for a visit was the occasion of great celebration, and a spree or convoy would be held in the family home and in the houses of friends and neighbours each night of the visitor's stay.

Most of the dance occasions previously mentioned refer to rural areas, but, of course, house dances were also a part of urban life much as a party in a house would be today. I have first hand accounts of half-sets being danced in the Duleek Gate area of Drogheda town where the speaker, the late Jackie Rooney, remembers his aunt playing the melodeon for the dancers (c.1915).

All of the dance occasions mentioned so far have been indoors, but in fact the most popular venue for a dance in the summertime was

---

20   James Argue, I.F.C., vol. 1209, pp. 546–7.
21   From an interview with the collector, Seán Corcoran. 1989. I.T.M.A.

outdoors, whether at a crossroads, "on the green field on a bright night" or at the gates of the local Big House such as Gormanstown Castle in County Meath when the dancing took place on a specially built roadside platform known as a dancing deck. The dancing deck was a portable floor made of wooden boards nailed together and the surface was ideal for dancing.

Specially constructed dance platforms were known in some areas as "maypoles". This name is possibly a vestige of an older custom dating back to the seventeenth century when, in the north midlands, there was the custom of calling the outdoor dances which began to be held at this time of year "maypole dances" and of the setting up of a small pole called a maypole at the crossroads where the dance was held. In parts of the north of Ireland such as Carrickfergus, County Antrim, the young men brought in a young straight tree from the country and planted it as a maypole on May Day. "Having elected a king and queen, they danced round the May pole and then visited the houses of the chief inhabitants for contributions."[22] In Dublin also, the maypole custom survived into the 1830s, when "'All Dublin' turned out to Finglas upon May Day to witness the sports and revels of the people." These included running after a pig with a shaved and well-soaped tail, which was let loose in the middle of the throng; grinning through horse collars for tobacco; blindfolded men trying to catch a bell-ringer; and dancing reels, jigs and hornpipes. "In the evening the crowds collected around the May pole, where the boys and girls danced in a ring until a late hour."[23] By the twentienth century, the maypole occasion existed in name only.

"Dancing at the crossroads" has nowadays assumed the status of a cliché, but it is undoubtedly the most vivid memory of dancing in bygone days and is recalled in place names such as the the Rinky Cross (from the Irish *rince* (dance), on the Togher Road outside Drogheda, County Louth. Other place names which preserve the image of dancing are Skeheen-aranky, from *Sceichín an Rince* (the little bush of the dancing) near Temple-tenny in County Tipperary, and Ballinrink (*Baile an Rinnce* – the town of the

---

22   *Ulster Journal of Archaeology*, vol. iii (1855), p. 164.
23   Sir William Wilde, *Irish Popular Superstitions* (First published Dublin: 1852. This edition Dublin: Irish Academic Press Limited, 1979), pp. 62–3.

dancing) in County Meath.[24] At a house dance, pressure of space limited the dance to a half-set whereas the open-air venue afforded the opportunity to do the larger group dances. An account from County Louth describes such a gathering: "The prevailing dance in those days was the set dance. It was made up of eight couples and consisted of six figures. Oft-times there were three sets in swing in the road at one time and always there was gaiety and laughter."[25]

At Neddie's Cross in County Meath, where crowds of up to 500 gathered, there were "four sets of eight couples up at the one time".[26] Here again we have a sixteen-hand dance described as a set whereas the "set" is normally perceived as a dance for four couples. At these massive Meath gatherings they also danced the quadrilles, the Highland fling, and the three-hand reel. Exhibitions of step dancing were part of every outdoor dance, and noted dancers would be invited on special occasions. Sometimes, a raffle in aid of some poor person of the neighbourhood was held in conjunction with the dancing. A lamb, a goat or a pair of shoes were donated as prizes, and everyone attending the Sunday crossroads dance subscribed according to their means – a shilling, a sixpenny piece or a penny or two.

In Kerry, the crossroads dances in the 1800s began and ended with the "country dance" – "an country deireanach" – a rank of boys and girls for about a hundred yards of the road at both sides[27]. This form of longways dance "for as many as will" was ideally suited to outdoor dancing. We are told that in County Cork, around Enniskean, a "pattern"[28] at the crossroads long ago, "was finished up with the 'country dance'".[29] Interestingly, we are told that in the *Gaeltacht* areas of County Kerry at the turn of the twentieth century, the dances were "called" by the dancing master or, if he was not

---

24 I am indebted to Dr Seán Ó Cearnaigh of the Ordnance Survey, Ireland, for this information.

25 Mrs Brigid Howard, née Flanagan, Mosstown, Dunleer, as reported to me in 1986.

26 Joseph Madden (70), Robertstown, Co. Meath, 1949, coll. P.J. Gaynor, I.F.C., vol. 1162, p. 309.

27 Eibhlín Ní Mhurchú, *Ceol agus Rinnce Mo Cheantair Dúchais ó 1800–1880* (Baile an Fheirtéaraigh, Co Chiarraí: Oidhreacht Chorca Dhuibhne, 1990), p. 118.

28 As used here, meaning a purely secular dance event.

29 Seán Barry (69), Kilrush, Enniskean, Co. Cork, 1936, coll. Diarmuid Ó Cruadhlaoch, I.F.C., vol. 437, p. 313.

present, by the fiddler: ". . . *agus cé nach raibh faic an uair sin ach Gaolainn go léir, is i mBéarla a bhíodh an chaint nuair a beifí ag stiúrú na rincí* |and even though there was nothing but Irish spoken at that time, the dancing was called in English|. B*híodh* 'up the middle' *acu,* 'hands across', *agus* 'around your partner'."[30] The source of this importation of English dance terminology was undoubtedly the rural dancing masters who were the main conduit of dance fashion from the fashions of the upper classes to the repertoire of the ordinary people.

Any kind of harvesting or co-operative labour effort usually ended in a dance. In Sligo, crossroads dances were hosted by local farmers after the flax-scutching during which the girls who worked on the harvest lived in roadside camps. A *meitheal* or "coor"[31] (group of neighbours who joined together to harvest each others crops etc.) were rewarded with a dance. In the Donegal Gaeltacht this was known as a *fidiléir* (literally, "a fiddler"). In Boho, County Fermanagh, an enterprising local grocer had all his Christmas turkeys plucked by organising an annual "coor" in a large barn behind his shop culminating in a "Turkey-plucking Ball" at which "the drink and feathers flew", as a local songmaker put it.[32] In Longford:

> At a lonesome spot in the road, there used to be dances in the Summer evenings. At that dance there would be at least 300. Ally Dunne, an old woman, would be going around among the dancers selling whiskey at 2d a naggin. There would be men as pickets on the road, looking out for the R.I.C. so that Ally wouldn't be caught selling the whiskey. If the R.I.C. came, the dance would be scattered.[33]

Dances were held on virtually any flat surface from a ball alley to a large flat rocky outcrop or even, famously, on the ice of a frozen lake, but the most extraordinary account mentions dancing in the 1930s on large tombstones in the graveyard in Carrick-on-Bannow in County Wexford.[34] No

---

30   Micheál Ó Suilleabháin, Corca Dhuibhne, Co. Kerry, 1945, coll. Fionán Mac Coluim, I.F.C., vol. 1124, p. 102.
31   From the Gaelic *cómhar* – co-operation.
32   "The Turkey-plucking Ball" (song), Fermanagh, 1983, Seán Corcoran, private collection.
33   Patrick Deignan (73), Derawley, Ballinamuck, Co. Longford, 1956, coll. Jim Delaney, I.F.C., vol. 1458, p. 94.
34   Máire Cáit Ní Goch, 1935, coll. Tomás Ó Ciarda, I.F.C., vol. 107, p. 77.

doubt there was no disrespect intended in this. It was just that such a firm flat and resonant surface would have been hard to resist!

In certain western counties such as Mayo, Clare and Galway, there was an outdoor dance event called a "hurling". In some cases there was a hurling match before the dance, but other accounts indicate that the occasion mainly consisted of an attempt at matchmaking. A likely couple was "caught" or selected by the crowd, and if they agreed they presided over a series of dances and saw to collecting money for the musicians. There was great dismay if the chosen couple refused to combine for it meant that the plans for a series of dances would fall through. Apparently, these "hurling catches" often resulted in a wedding.

Weddings in general were celebrated with much dancing both in the future bride and groom's family homes and after the wedding in the couple's new home. A particular feature of some wedding dances was the abrupt arrival of strawboys, dressed in suits and masks of straw, who used their disguise as a licence to engage in all sorts of "jig-acting". It is said that occasionally a disappointed suitor of the bride would vent his spleen under cover of his straw mask. Such an intruder would often roughly claim a dance with the bride, even when she was unwilling. Tricks with sexual innuendo were often played, and since custom forbade the hosts to refuse hospitality to the intruders, an uncomfortable situation could arise until the strawboys finally melted away into the night.

These dance occasions which are now but a memory are looked back on with great fondness by all those who participated in them. The death of the country house dances is bitterly felt and their epitaph could well be written in the words of the late Junior Crehan of Mullagh, west Clare: "The country house was our school where we learned to play music and dance and it was a crying shame it was closed against the country people."[35]

Voices from all over the country would undoubtedly echo Junior's heartfelt statement. A way of life is now no more. Its demise was not gradual and natural. On the contrary, it was brutally and prematurely ended. All the more reason to lament its passing.

---

35   Larry Lynch, *Set Dances of Ireland: Tradition and Evolution* (Miltown Malbay, Co. Clare: Séadna Books, in collaboration with Dal gCais Publications, 1989), p. 43.

Chapter Eight

"The Hobs of Hell": The Clergy and Irish Dance

Priest to parishioner:	Am I to understand that, in spite of my warning against it, you attended a dance at Bun na Leice crossroads?
Parishioner:	I did, Father.
Priest:	I hope you know, my good man, that you were dancing there on the Hobs of Hell.
Parishioner:	Aye, well if I was, Father, it was very cheery.[1]

THROUGHOUT HISTORY, MANY if not most of the Irish clergy were implacably opposed to dancing. The people, however, were quietly but firmly determined to follow their own will in the matter. As early as 1660, the Synod of Tuam decreed: "*Prohibentur tripudia, tibicines, symphoniae, commisationes et allii abusus in visitatione fontium et aliorum sacrorum locorum.*" ("Dancing, flute-playing, bands of music, riotous revels and other abuses in visiting holy wells and other holy places are forbidden.")[2] In 1777 we find the Cashel bishops giving exemplary punishments for dancing, while in 1803 Bishop Plunkett of Meath condemned Sunday dancing.[3] Despite such opposition, dancing continued unabated.

---

1   Breandán Bonnar, Na Glaisigh, Co. Donegal, 1989. Verbal communication.
2   Caoimhin Ó Danachair, "The Death of a Tradition", *Studies* (Autumn 1974), p. 222.
3   S. J. Connolly, *Priests and People in Pre-Famine Ireland* (Dublin: Gill and Macmillan, 1982), p. 168.

An account from County Wexford gives an insight into clerical attitudes to dance in the late 1890s:

There was a priest in Rathangan about forty years ago by the name of Father W. He was a very holy man and was awfully strict on boys and girls. He would go around the roads with a big stick in the night time. He wouldn't allow dances at all. One time there was a set of mummers started in Rathangan, and they were partly afraid to start for they thought he would be putting a stop to them. The priest heard of the mummers alright, but said nothing, only he wouldn't allow them to have any ball and they would have to finish up every night at ten o'clock. They were satisfied enough with that. They mummed for about three months and then it was into the New Year and it was time for them to leave it so. Some of them said it would be a pity they couldn't wind up with a ball. They all came to the conclusion that it would be worth anything to have a whole night's fun. They decided to carry out the ball unknown to the priest. They would have a good night anyhow and the priest could say what he liked afterwards. So all preparations were made and the night of the ball came. The priest had a boy working with him and he was also going to the ball. The ball was to start about eight o'clock. The priest's boy was eating his supper at the kitchen when Father Williams came in and he was in an awful rage. "I hear," he says, "there's going to be a ball down at Murphys' to-night and I want you to stay here and mind the place for I'm going down there to put a stop to their little game." "Well," says the boy, "I want to go home and give a few shillings to my mother, but I'll be back to mind the place until you come back from Murphys."

The priest consented and the boy went off – but it wasn't thinking of his mother he was but of the night's fun being in danger. So he went with all haste to the ballroom. No one had arrived for the ball only about six or eight and they were in the kitchen laughing and talking when the priest's boy entered. He told them the priest was coming down at eight o'clock. A couple of fellows went up to the end of the lane and stopped all the people from coming and all the girls hid in the parlour. There was a short cut from the priest's house to Murphy's, so there was no danger of the priest coming up the lane.

When it struck eight o'clock all the members of the Murphys knelt down and started to say the Rosary, and when they were just finishing who comes in only the priest. He stood looking around from one to the other for about two minutes and then walked out. He couldn't believe his eyes. He thought sure and he coming across the fields to the house that he would find them all in the barn, and they dancing and carrying-on to their hearts content, but instead all was quiet and the family saying the Rosary. The priest went home and got into the bed and never said a word about dances until the day he died. When he was gone and the Rosary was finished the girls came down out of the parlour and all the rest of the company collected, and they lit the lights in the barn, and if they hadn't a good nights fun it's a queer thing.[4]

This light-hearted humorous treatment of the matter overlays a much darker reality. A commentator writing in 1912 tells us:

The heart and spirit gave way in a sort of terrorism before the priest. In his day of dominance, he did much to make Irish local life a dreary desert. He waged war on the favourite cross-roads dances – with exceptions here and there – and on other gatherings where young men and women congregated in the company of their older relations and friends.[5]

From all parts of the country come first-hand accounts of priests opposing the holding of informal dances. During the heyday of clerical opposition in the 1920s, "Wooden road-side platforms were set on fire by curates; surer still, the priests drove their cars backwards and forwards over the timber platforms; concertinas were sent flying into hill streams and those who played music at dances were branded as outcasts."[6]

Occasionally, clerical disapproval took a sacramental form. Those who defied the priest could be given public penance. In the late 1800s, a mother and daughter from the Glens of Antrim were put under a penance for dancing. "Their penance was that they had to walk barefooted to Ballymena and if I'm not mistaken walk home the same way. Whenever a Glens cart would be coming they'd be very mad about it, trying to hide you may be sure."[7]

A story is told in County Donegal of a priest who used to grab the shawls off women he found dancing at a crossroads dance. He brought

---

4   Ned Gough, Woodgraigue, Duncormick, Co. Wexford, 1936, coll. Seán De Buitléir, Irish Folklore Commission, vol. 172, pp.35-8.
5   W.P. Ryan, *The Pope's Green Island* (London: J. Nisbet, 1912), p. 78.
6   Bryan Mac Mahon, *The Vanishing Ireland* (Dublin: O'Brien Press, 1954), p. 212.
7   Frank McAuley, Layde, Co. Antrim, 1952, coll. Michael J. Murphy, I.F.C., vol. 1356, p. 18.

them to the parochial house so that he could interrogate and give a penance to each woman as she came to claim her shawl. However, he reckoned without his housekeeper who would secretly return the women's shawls to them, through the back door of the parochial house.[8]

Another form of social pressure applied by some priests was the threat to refuse a reference to a parishioner who attended a dance proscribed by them.

Musicians who played for the dance were also a target. In Kerry, I was told of an instance when a local priest refused absolution to a musician he saw playing at a dance in the 1930s to put pressure on him to stop.[9] So deep was the hurt and alienation felt by some musicians at their treatment that many of them left Ireland for good. Captain Francis O'Neill, the noted collector of Irish dance music, and himself a traditional musician, met many such men in America. Writing to Fr Séamus O'Floinn of Cork in 1916, he says:

Not few are the pipers and fiddlers thus forced into exile by the unwarrantable harshness of the clergy who never outgrew the bitterness arising from their experience and to such a degree had the sense of wrong rankled in their breasts that some now in Chicago and in the enjoyment of prosperity decline to figure on the programmes of church entertainments.[10]

Such was the fear engendered by the priest's perceived power that his authority was rarely challenged. Occasionally, however, he might meet outright opposition. A story is still told in west Clare about the travelling dancing master Pat Barron, who persisted in teaching dancing and holding dances in a disused house despite the priest's disapproval. One day the priest threatened him: "If you don't cease to promote dancing in my parish against my express wishes, I will have no alternative but to turn you into a goat." Quick as a flash Barron replied, "If you do, Father, the first thing I'll do will be to puck you in the arse."[11]

---

8   Breandán Bonnar, Na Glaisigh, Co. Donegal, 1989. Video interview.
9   Johnny O'Leary, Gneeveguilla, Co. Kerry, 1985. Verbal communication.
10 Breandán Breathnach, *Dancing in Ireland* (Miltown Malbay, Co. Clare: Dal gCais, 1983), p. 47. The original letter is in the library of Notre Dame University, Indiana, USA.
11 Martin ("Junior") Crehan, Mullagh, Co. Clare. Verbal communication during a field trip to Clare in 1984.

Because the dancing masters were often the focus of dance activity in an area, they bore the brunt of clerical disapproval. Johnny Leary "kept dance schools" in the Kilrush district of County Cork in "any old vacant house that he could get . . . It was often very hard on him because the priests often objected to his dance schools."[12]

In the 1920s the Church leaders' opposition to dancing focused on condemnation of privately run dance halls. The Catholic archbishops and bishops of Ireland issued a statement on the "evils of dancing" on 6 October 1925, which was to be read at masses during the Ecclesiastical Year. They advocated the strict supervision of dancing and warned of the "occasions of sin" involved in night dances: "Given a few frivolous young people in a locality and a few careless parents and the agents of the wicked one will come and do the rest."[13]

An *Irish Times* editorial of 2 March 1929 echoed the bishops' statement.

The clergy, the judges and the police are in agreement concerning the baleful affects of drink and low dancing upon rural morals. Further restrictions on the sale of drinks, a remorseless war on the poteen industry, the strict supervision of dance halls and the banning (by law if need be) of all night dances would abolish many inducements to sexual vice.

Another target of the moralists was "imported dances of an evil kind", or so-called "dubious dances". The bishops' pastoral of 1925 urged the populace to confine themselves to "Irish" dances, which have as one of their chief merits that "they cannot be danced for long hours . . . They may not be the fashion in London or Paris. They should be the fashion in Ireland." Giving their apostolic seal of approval they conclude: "Irish dances do not make degenerates."

The paternalistic and nationalistic tone of many pronouncements on the "evils of dancing" echoed through the 1920s and 1930s, a period of civil and political strife in Ireland. Finally, in 1935, the government passed a bill – the Public Dance Hall Act – which confined the holding of dances to halls licensed for such a purpose and which imposed a government tax on

---

12 Seán Barry (69), Kilrush, Enniskean, Co. Cork, 1936–7, coll. Diarmuid Ó Cruadhlaoich, I.F.C., vol. 437, p. 313.

13 *Irish Ecclesiastical Record*, vol. XXVII (Dublin: Browne and Nolan Ltd., Jan–June, 1926), p. 9.

the admission price. All over rural Ireland, the clergy organised the construction of parochial halls, and thereafter Church and state combined to eliminate the organisation of any dances outside these halls.

Police raids on house dances became common, one excuse being that money was possibly being charged at the door in contravention of the law. The noted Clare musician and storyteller Junior Crehan, who himself played at many a house dance, tells us:

> They believed that there was immoral conduct carried out at the country houses and that there was no sanitary arrangements. That was their excuse. You had to pay three pence tax to the shilling going into the hall which meant money to the Government. They didn't care if you made your water down the chimney as long as they collected their money.[14]

In 1935 and the following year, a spate of court cases connected with the Dance Hall Act took place. In an area such as County Clare, where the practice of holding house dances was deeply rooted, the effect of the new legislation was particularly noticeable. The influence of the clergy extended to attempting to persuade judges to stop or limit Saturday night dancing because otherwise the people might not attend mass and also to impose a geographical limit beyond which outsiders could not attend local dances. In one such instance, reported in the *Clare Champion* of 5 October 1935, the parish priest of Kilkee, County Clare, appealed to the district justice at Kilrush Circuit Court as follows:

> There was a dance held at Moynasta some time ago and it was a disgrace . . . The dances held in country districts were attended by boys and girls from a distance of 12, 14 or perhaps 15 miles and what could a person expect in such a little place in a country house with people from all sorts of places. They have no "hawks" and these are the people we want curbed and the only way of doing this is by restricting the area. [He corrects this report in a letter the following week to "They are not motorhawks." They came from the four winds on bicycles."]

---

14 Larry Lynch, *Set Dances of Ireland. Tradition and Evolution*, (Miltown Malbay, Co. Clare: Séadna Books, in collaboration with Dal gCais Publications, 1989), p. 43.

He regrets that the judge was too "liberal": "I trust that public opinion will help to modify his views in such matters."

On 19 October, a letter in the same newspaper from "Exile on the Continent" declares that the "dance craze rampant in Clare and Ireland is both scandalous and mystifying . . . Even in Paris or Monte Carlo where there are dens of vice dances would never continue to 5 a.m."[15]

The first prosecution in Clare under the Dance Hall Act was in November 1935. The case was reported under the heading;

KILKEE COURT

TALE OF THE FLUTE PLAYERS

'A BOB A HEAD'

KEEPING OUT THE COUNTRY BOYS.

M.M. of Kilkee was summoned for holding a dance contrary to the Dance Hall regulations.

Sergeant Carroll stated that on the 1st of August he was on duty in Kilkee in civilian attire and was accompanied by Guard Kiernan. When passing the defendant's house he heard music and noise as if a dance were in progress. He went to the door and it was opened by a man called M.M. who greeted the witness with words, "Pay up: bob a head". Witness paid 1/– and went in and found five boys and five girls sitting around the kitchen. There were two flute players present. Mrs M. was also present. When approached she claimed the dance was free and "that she had told the man on the door that if any 'country boys' came to say that the charge was 1/– per head, just to keep them out."

The judge imposed a fine of £3 reduced to £2 on the appeal of Sergeant Carroll who said that the defendant was a very poor man.[16]

As stated elsewhere, it was not uncommon for poorer families to run dances in their homes for which admission was charged in an attempt to supplement their income. The conviction in the Kilkee case showed that the new legislation made this practice illegal. However, the reports of prosecutions under the Dance Hall Act show that even private functions

15   *Clare Champion*, 19 October 1935.
16   *Ibid.*, 9 November 1935.

such as a dance given by a farmer for the workers who had helped him save his crops were to be subject to licence. It can be seen from these reports that even the judge appears to be somewhat mystified by some of the ramifications of the new act.

M.W. of Shanaway West was summoned for having a dance in his house without first having obtained a licence.

> Sergeant Murphy said that he had not been at the dance himself but after the dance he went to the defendant's house and having cautioned him he made a statement admitting that he had held a dance at which 26 girls and 40 boys attended. There was no charge for admission and tea was supplied at the defendant's expense. He got up the dance for his neighbours who had helped him to save the crops.[17]

The case was dismissed.

D.D. of Dunsallagh was also summoned for holding a similar dance without a licence.

> Sergeant Murphy said he took a statement from the defendant who admitted giving a dance to the boys and girls who had helped him with the turf and potatoes. The Justice asked the Superintendent why the case had been brought at all when there was no question of payment. The Superintendent said that if dances were allowed in houses of this sort without licence everyone could attend for miles around and the Act would be defeated altogether. If he heard there was a dance in a country house there was nothing to prevent him going if these things were allowed to go on. The defendant said he was ignorant of the law on the matter or he would not have allowed the dance. He gave an undertaking to the court that he would not offend in that respect again.

The justice found the charge proved and, dismissing it, said that "this type of dance was absolutely illegal and in future there would be severe penalties for getting up a dance such as the dance in the present case and in the previous case too, probably. It would be the last of those cases that would be dismissed under the circumstances."[18]

---

17 Ibid., 14 December 1935.
18 Ibid.

A further instance in which the 1935 act made inroads into long-established social custom and practice was a prosecution for holding a "gamble" – a night of card-playing with prizes for the winners, which was particularly popular coming up to Christmas. It seemed that even such domestic festivity was not immune from prosecution.

In Ennis District Court on 10 January 1936, M.K. of Clonbooly was summoned for having a dance in his house. "A gamble for turkeys was also held in the defendant's house on the 11th December." The guests paid 1/- each for the gamble. When the gamble was over, they took part in a dance which finished about 4am. About thirty people attended and there were three turkeys. The man of the house provided tea with bread, butter and jam. The defendant said that his daughter had asked for a few "sets" and he agreed. Superintendent Keenan said similar things were happening all over the locality. The justice said it was happening in every locality in the county. The defendant was found guilty and the Probation Act applied.[19]

The 1 February 1936 edition of the *Clare Champion* contains a report from Sixmilebridge Court which provides an unusual insight into the tensions which were beginning to surface around the operation of the Dance Hall Act. In open court, the justice makes the following remarks:

> "It was a very invidious thing for the Parish Priest to write to me and say that
> if I granted any more licences I would hear more about it. I hope I will get
> no more letters of that description from that quarter or from any other
> quarter either."

Such a public rebuke must have caused raised eyebrows in court, at the very least.

The year 1936 saw a continuation of prosecutions under the act. The long-established practice of running informal house dances was not easily relinquished and the interference of the state in domestic merrymaking continued to be challenged. A widow living in Cooraclare was summoned in February after the sergeant was passing her house at 1.30am and saw a lot of bicycles and heard music. In the kitchen there were about thirty persons. Some present had come from long distances,

---

19   *Ibid.*, 10 January 1936.

as far as Kilmihil, some twelve miles. A set was in progress, dancing to the music of a flute played by a young chap who was sitting in the corner. There was no one at the door and no charge. The defendant held dances regularly in her house, before and after the act. She did not charge as she had no need of money. She ran dances for neighbours who helped her with her farm.

The judge expressed surprise that:

> . . . this lady, whose dancing days in the natural order of things should be over, had organised a dance and invited people there. She was not very flush in the world's goods; still she could bring people there and have a dance in her house. He could not see what amusement she got from watching people dance up to 2 am when she should be in her bed.

The judge's bewilderment was addressed by the solicitor for the defence, Mr T.F. Twomey, who told the judge that "it was a general thing in the country to set a house or two aside for this sort of thing and the defendant's house was suitable and was one of these houses. As a rule people did not frequent houses where there were young children."

The judge is still unclear as to why the defendant – an elderly woman – should wish to be out of her bed at such a late hour watching dancers, and demands an explanation. Her solicitor continues that "she did dance in her day herself and on this occasion it was Christmas time and it was nothing unusual to have a dance up to that hour. On the occasion of the Sergeant's visit, the dance in progress was the last dance of the night."

Various witnesses who were present on the night were called and a spirited defence of the night's fun was mounted. It was stated that "all the people who attended were present on the invitation of some member of the family", contrary to the evidence of the sergeant who had maintained that it was an "open" dance. The judge, in his summing-up, said that the legislature never intended that a person could not invite a few neighbours to his house for the purpose of having a dance. He dismissed the prosecution.[20] This judgement was important in that it finally recognised the nature of many informal nights of social dance which had been severely curtailed by less liberal interpretations of the act. Notably, the defendant

---

20   *Ibid.*, 22 February, 1936.

in the case was at pains to state that she was not running the dance for economic reasons. This was one of the factors which swayed the judge's decision to acquit her.

Contrary to the perceived notion of County Clare in this period as being entirely composed of cosy homesteads and well-stocked barns, the reality was that unemployment and poverty were rife in both rural and urban areas. Initiatives by the local authorities to alleviate appalling overcrowding in towns such as Kilrush and Ennis, described as "slum clearances" by the contemporary local press, were constantly in the news. An issue of the *Clare Champion* of 1936 refers to a demonstration of the unemployed led by bands in Ennis to demand relief[21] and records heated scenes at the December meeting of Clare County Council when 300 unemployed men pleaded for Christmas dinner for their families.[22] In this context, it is not surprising that when Mr P.C. of Considine Terrace, Ennis, applied for a licence in September 1936 to hold a dance in his house because "he was out of work and wanted to pay his rent", the judge granted him an 8pm to 12am licence because of his situation.

However, in some quarters, the economic climate was secondary to the perceived danger to the moral health of the nation. Opposing a proposal to hold a regatta dance in Courtmacsherry, the local parish priest declares:

> Revolution and the overthrow of law and order do not happen overnight but are the result of long sapping and mining the foundations of Christian behaviour. Immorality and impiety are the twin dangers which Christianity must overcome in the new world which is now in the making.

> Is it not a moment for us in Ireland to weaken any of our defences, to make light of the immodest dance, the startlingly nudist costumes that confront one in every street, the still more flagrant nudist bathing costumes on every seashore.[23]

The controversy surrounding the morality of dancing continued into the 1940s and is reflected in views such as the following, published by the

---

21 *Ibid.*, 12 September 1936.
22 *Ibid.*, 12 December 1936.
23 *Ibid.*, 5 September 1936.

Gaelic Athletic Association. Condemning many foreign dances as "negroid imitations", the writer, who may have been expressing a personal view, recommends the promotion of Irish dances in that "It is a fundamental characteristic of Irish dancing that the nearest approach to contiguity is the joining of outstretched hands. They should secure universal and parental approval."[24] The dances referred to in this context are the group dances fostered by the Gaelic League which were confined to organised *céilithe*. The popular dances of the period were the sets, which were dismissed by the Gaelic League as "foreign dances".

In a typically irreverent account of the dance customs deriving from the notion of dance as an ideological battleground, the writer Flann O'Brien proclaims:

> Irish dancing is a thing apart. There is perhaps one "céilidhe" held for every twenty dances. The foxtrot and the Fairy Reel are mutually repugnant and will not easily dwell under the same roof. Very few adherents of the "ballroom" canon will have anything to do with a jig or a reel. Apart from the fact that the Irish dance is ruled out in most halls by considerations of space or perspiration, there is a real psychological obstacle. It is a very far cry from the multiple adhesion of enchanted country stomachs in a twilight of coloured bulbs to the impersonal free-for-all of a clattering reel. Irish dancing is emotionally cold, unromantic and always well-lighted.

O'Brien, moreover, was well aware of the toing and froing involved in the administration of the 1935 Dance Hall Act:

> Some district justices have a habit of taking leave of their senses at the annual licensing sessions. They want Irish dancing and plenty of it, even at the most monster "gala dance." They believe that Satan with all his guile is baffled by a four-hand reel and cannot make head or tail of the Rakes of Mallow. I do not think that there is any real ground for regarding Irish dance as a sovereign spiritual and nationalistic prophylactic.[25]

The iconoclastic views of Flann O'Brien were probably not very well received in official circles at the time, but they could, in retrospect, be

---

24   Joseph Aurelius, "National Action", published by the Gaelic Athletic Association (1943).
25   Flann O'Brien, "The Dance Halls", in *The Bell* (1941), pp. 51–2.

seen as providing an antidote to the painful political process which under-lay the turbulent years of the 1930s. The passing of the 1935 act seriously damaged the control of the people over the organisation of dancing which was one of their favourite forms of entertainment. However, it did not suc-ceed in entirely eliminating the sense of genuine "crack", as the following story shows. The writer, belying his skills as a raconteur, tells us, "I am a farmer and put a farmer at anything but not the pen."

The tale concerns a piper called Jimmy Fallon, who played at all the local weddings and American wakes. He was blind from his early days owing to smallpox.

One day this Jimmy Fallon was playing his pipes at a dance on a ballalley, the time of day was 3 o'clock. Everyone was enjoying the fun. This ballalley was on the bank of a lake and the wind being blowing in the right (or wrong!) direction the parish priest heard the music and this man was very much against dancing even in the daylight. So he got his blackthorn stick and set sail on foot guided by the piper and his music. Near the alley there was a sharp bend in the byroad and the priest was spotted in time. There was a fine young girl in the crowd who understood the plight of the piper. As for the rest of them they could run away. She was very fond of dancing and to get a piper to play on a ballalley was something to look forward to. She made one dive for the piper, picked him up, pipes and all, and headed for the lake and carried him on her shoulder through water, mud and rushes to the other side followed by the rest of the crowd, a distance of 500 yards. On that side of the lake was a green hill. There they set up the piper and he never played better music in his life before and everyone danced for the whole day all in their wet clothes. The priest stood on the other side wav-ing his blackthorn stick and shouting if he could get across what he wouldn't do. The dancers waved their caps and shawls in return and the priest went home a vexed man. The dance went on and no pains in the bones next day. They were the good old days, never again to return, God be with them all.[26]

Agus fágaimíd siúd mar atá sé, in ainm Chroim. ("And we'll leave it at that, in the name of all that's holy.")

---

26 Thomas Kelly, Grange, Curraghboy, Athlone, Co. Westmeath, 1969, I.F.C. dance questionnaire.

Chapter Nine

From Johnny to Jiveáil:
Focus on a Dance Community

I N THE REGION of Connemara on the west coast of Galway, where the very
fields have had to be created by back-breaking labour, where the life of
the sea is in the people's blood and where the Irish language is still the
primary means of communication, there exists a world of dance which
incorporates the ancient and the modern in a unique and fascinating way.

In Connemara, the most popular dances are the set or half-set, the
"Johnny" and solo dances such as the reel, jig and hornpipe. Also very popular amongst the younger age group is *jiveáil* (jiving) – which is danced in
a very individual way with the skilled footwork of the *damhsa aonair* (solo
dance) being applied to the American import. Indeed, it is almost a tru-
ism that the young prizewinners of the solo dance competitions in the
area will always be expert (and enthusiastic) jivers. The older age group
prefer the *válsáil* (waltzing). The dance events in Connemara now revolve
around the pub whereas up to the 1970s anyone attempting to dance in a
pub would most likely have been shown the door if he didn't desist. At
local house dances, solo performances were always interspersed between
group dances and solo singing.

Generally a dancer would begin to dance as if moved to do so by a favourite tune played with "lift" – a rhythmic effect produced by a musician who understands the local dance style and can inspire the dancers. Initially, the dancer performs alone. Soon, he is joined by another. They beat out the rhythm, dancing now separately, now opposite one another, each dancer's performance sparking off an ever more energetic display in his companion. More and more dancers join the fray as they feel moved by the excitement of the music and challenged by the performance of the dancers already on the floor.

This type of spontaneous display is rare nowadays. The dance arena has moved from the country house to the public house, and the dance occasion usually takes the form of a *comórtas ar a sean-nós* – a dance competition. Following the announcement of the results of the competition, it is common for all the participants to get up to dance together, and they may be joined by any member of the audience who wishes to do so. And so this dance style still has its informal side.

The recognition accorded to the *sean-nós* dance since the 1970s is in marked contrast to its position prior to this when it was seen as a loose, unstructured form, unrecognised and unsanctified by the arbiters of Irish national dance practice, *An Coimisiún le Rinncí Gaelacha*. The elevation by *An Coimisiún* of the southern style into the "national" style and the consigning of any other regional styles, such as the northern or western styles, to virtual oblivion, resulted in the marginalisation of these local styles of dance. Outside the Connemara *Gaeltacht* the *sean-nós* style was unknown, and even within the *Gaeltacht* the *Coimisiún* style, locally called *damhsa foghlamtha* (learned dance), was accorded higher cultural status. An elderly dancer told me that the *sean-nós* style was perceived by many as, "what the boys got up to when the dancing master's back was turned". Its emphasis on individual expression is in marked contrast to the method followed by the *damhsa foghlamtha* dancer which demands strict adherence to a prescribed code of practice.

The most popular forms in solo dancing in Connemara are the reel and the jig. Also danced are *damhsa na scuaibe* (the brush dance) and *damhsa na gcoiníní* (the rabbits' dance). The reel, as a dance form, originally incorporated a reeling or figure-of-eight movement of which there is some evidence in Ireland generally. However, in Connemara the reel in the *sean-nós* style simply applies the local style of stepping to the reel tempo, with its characteristic bars of 8 quavers. Even where two or more dancers hold the floor at the same time, they do not relate to one another in any pre-planned formation, whether reeling or otherwise.

Although Connemara musicians – mainly accordeonists or "box players" – are as musically accomplished as those in any other area, they are aware that when playing for the solo *sean-nós* dancer they will be expected, indeed they may be called upon, to play one of a very limited number of tunes. The majority of dancers will call for "Miss McLeod's Reel" played at a very brisk speed.

The jig is rarely danced nowadays in this tradition, although popular in former times. Many older people speak of dancers such as the late Tomás Cheaite Breathnach of Carna and Pádraic Bradley of Rosmuc, whose repertoire included all three popular dance tempos: the reel, the jig and the hornpipe. The most popular jig tune for the Connemara dancer is "The Lark in the Morning" while the favoured hornpipe was "The Boys of Blue Hill".

Damhsa na scuaibe is one of a group of dances in the Irish tradition which combine stepping with a display of athleticism and precision of movement requiring balance and dexterity. In Connemara an ordinary sweeping brush is incorporated into the dance. In other areas, as we have seen, crossed sticks, crossed handkerchiefs, a belt or a cross marked on the floor with a burnt stick provide the necessary props. Whereas the movements and structure of the dance vary from area to area, the element of body control and precision of footwork is common to this family of dances. The dancer begins by entering on to the dance floor pushing the sweeping brush before him or her. He advances and retires, accompanied by the brush, dancing his favourite reel steps. Then, without missing a beat, he drops the brush and proceeds to dance a series of steps, hither and over the handle of the brush. At the end of this phase, he must, again without missing a beat, pick up the brush and recommence the sweeping movement around the perimeter of the floor.

The final flourish is a real test of agility and athleticism. The dancer holds the handle of the brush in one hand at an angle of 60 degrees from the floor. He then swings first one leg, then the other over the brush handle in rapid succession, the brush handle changing from hand to hand, while keeping time with the music. This sequence takes up 8 bars of the music, with usually two leg-swings per bar and the final test would be to attempt four swings per bar! Finally, he exits as he entered, pushing the brush before him. This dance is a highly popular feature of a night's dancing wherever Connemara people gather. Nowadays, it is often performed during the break after a competition, while the adjudicator is making up his or her mind. To date, it is seen purely as entertainment and inappropriate for competition purposes.

The final dance in the local repertoire is one of a category known to dance anthropologists as squat-fling dances. It is called locally *damhsa na gcoiníní* (the rabbits' dance). The performer gets down on his hunkers; he shoots one leg out straight, then, quickly drawing it back he shoots the other leg out, and so on around the floor. This type of dance is found in many regions of Europe. According to Curt Sachs: "The Greeks who took this dance from the Persians knew it as 'Oklasma'; carvings show the Etruscans had it."[1] This dance is performed in Connemara without musical accompaniment and is generally regarded locally as more a *teist aclaíochta* (an athletic test) than a bona fide dance.

Whilst the solo dance style of Connemara is part of the body of vernacular step dance which is still practised in many parts of Ireland, it has certain characteristics which distinguish it from other styles. For instance, the *sean-nós* dancer does not necessarily attempt to "cover the floor" (i.e. use as much as possible of the dancing area available). Most steps are danced "in place". A recent *Oireachtas* title-holder, Máirtín Mac Donnacha of Ráth Chairn, whose parents originally came from Connemara, for want of a plate, occasionally dances on a dartboard!

The body posture of the dancer is erect but relaxed. Swaying movements of the body to left and right may be used. Dancers may move their shoulders in time with the music. Arms are held loosely and may occasionally be raised to shoulder height or even higher.

The foot position is generally similar to normal walking movements. Stamping movements are common. Characteristic of this style is a form of

---

1   Curt Sachs, *World History of the Dance* (New York: W.W. Norton & Company, Inc., 1963), p. 30.

heel-and-toe stepping. Sequences of steps are not fixed. Dancers will develop their own repertoire of steps from the step-elements in their own tradition, and each dancer's performance will be highly individualistic.

The tempo of the accompanying music is as fast as, if not slightly faster than, a similar tune played for group social dances. As one dancer told me, "*Ní féidir é a dhéanamh mall.*" ("It can't be done slowly.") Reel tempo is by far the favourite with Connemara dancers, followed by the hornpipe and occasional jig. Dancers will often favour a specific tune for their performances and will request it from the musicians before they dance.

The dancer in the *sean-nós* style wears no particular footwear or costume. Some dancers wear soft-soled shoes, whereas others maintain that the characteristic heel-and-toe tapping requires leather-soled footwear. It is entirely unknown for a dancer in this style to wear anything other than normal everyday dress. Female dancers, particularly younger women, tend to wear trousers rather than skirts, on the basis that this allows greater freedom of movement.

Prior to the introduction of organised competitions, the *sean-nós* style was male dominated, although women were not excluded from performing. This seems to have been the norm in traditional solo step dancing in all areas of the country. However, many male dancers in Connemara cite the dancing of their mothers in the home as a major influence. Nowadays competitions are often won by women but they still constitute a minority of participants. However, Annie Ní Dhúbháin, a well-known *sean-nós* dancer from Carna in west Connemara, who has initiated the formal teaching of the style to youngsters in the area, asserts that more girls are keen to learn than boys: "*Tá na cailíní ag teacht aníos anois agus is maith an scéal é sin – go bhfuil na mná ag déanamh níos fearr ná na fir.*" ("The girls are coming on now and that's a good thing – that the women are doing better than the men.")[2]

In the *sean-nós* style, performance is still generally informal and spontaneous except for the recent development of competitions, but these often have a great air of informality about them, being locally based and lacking the bureaucratic features of the Irish Dancing Commission's competitions. Competitors will often refuse to submit their names until the last

---

2   Annie Ní Dhúbháin, Carna, Connemara. Personal communication.

minute, thus retaining the element of spontaneous performance inherent in the tradition. The popularity of *jiveáil* (jiving) and *válsáil* (waltzing) in the area has meant that the annual dance competitions during Pléaráca Chonamara (Connemara Revels) – the annual festival in September – include these dances by popular demand.

The development of these Connemara-based *sean-nós* dancing competitions is rooted in the chequered history of the "language question" and its central position in Irish cultural politics. *Conradh na Gaeilge*, with its urban-based, language-revivalist policies, has not always been looked upon kindly by people in the *Gaeltachtaí*. In the late 1960s a group of activists in the Connemara *Gaeltacht* founded *Gluaiseacht Chearta Síbhialta na Gaeltachta* (the *Gaeltacht* Civil Rights Movement). One of its members expressed the frustration of many in the *Gaeltacht* when he said, "The revivalists and language enthusiasts regarded the *Gaeltachtaí* in some mystical romantic way as special holy places which should not be desecrated by modernism and development."[3]

Essentially, the *Gaeltacht* Civil Rights Movement resented the fact that the annual gathering of the League – An tOireachtas, which is a mixture of social events and competitions – was always held in Dublin and felt that its preoccupations were remote from the realities of *Gaeltacht* life. Such was the groundswell of support for these criticisms that it was decided in 1975 to hold the *Oireachtas* in Cois Fharraige in Connemara. It soon became apparent, however, that merely relocating the event would not alter its basically urban middle-class cultural values. Events such as the elaborate Fáiltiú (Welcoming) Dinner Dance and a weekend of choral singing competitions held little appeal for the people of the Connemara *Gaeltacht*.

In response to this, the Civil Rights activists decided to organise a fringe event – an exhibition of old-style solo step dancing by local people. According to Máirtín Jaimsie Ó Flaithearta of Raidió Na Gaeltachta, himself a fine dancer in this style, the term *damhsa ar an sean-nós* was first used of the dancing at this event. *Sean-nós* had been accepted as a term to describe the intricate local style of solo unaccompanied singing, and its connotations

---

3   Donncha Ó hÉallaithe, "The Gaeltacht – Myth and Reality", in *The Irish Reporter*, vol. 11 (third quarter, 1993), p. 3.

would be readily understood both inside and outside the *Gaeltachtaí*. The presentation of *sean-nós* dancing during the *Oireachtas '75* was an important element in the desire to highlight one of the distinctive features of Connemara culture which was unrecognised by, and probably unknown to, the authorities of the Gaelic League. The programme of the official *Oireachtas* had never allowed for the inclusion of this type of popular dance commonly found at social gatherings in Connemara.

It is a measure of the success of this initiative that in 1977 the programme of the official *Oireachtas* included, for the first time, a competition for *sean-nós* dancing. A recent holder of the title is Máirtín Mac Donnacha, from the Ráth Cairn *Gaeltacht*, in County Meath, whose family originally come from Connemara. However, the focus of the development of *sean-nós* dancing competitions has been in the *Gaeltachtaí* themselves. In Ráth Cairn, for instance, a major event is held each New Year's Eve, and in Connemara the high point of the dancer's calender is in September when *Pléaráca Chonamara* takes place.

The lead-up to this event is interesting. It began, effectively, in 1990 when *Bord na Gaeilge*, the official government department concerned with Irish language affairs, commissioned the writer Breandán Ó hEithir, a native of Inis Mór, Aran, to write a report on the condition of the Irish language. The report apparently alarmed the authorities; it was never published but was leaked to the press. One of the central tenets of the report was that the failure of government policies for the *Gaeltachtaí* in the 1980s had produced demoralisation and a lack of faith in local self-organisation, and that the people of the *Gaeltacht* had "no confidence in their own culture".[4] Stung by this, a new generation of local activists in Connemara developed a set of economic, social and cultural initiatives, and from this came the highly successful *Pléaráca*, a week-long festival including music, song, storytelling, drama, dance and sport.

One of the event's organisers, Donncha Ó hÉallaithe, a well-known commentator on cultural events in Connemara, says: "*Pléaráca* was organised to show that Connemara isn't dead culturally. It is a reaction against a view that was common on the east coast, among the Irish

---

4   *Irish Times*, 21 March 1994.

language movement particularly, that Connemara as a *Gaeltacht* was dead. *Pléaráca* started off as a celebration of everything that was involved in south Connemara culture."[5]

When preparing publicity material, it was felt that the visual element required an image which was "lively" and which would "speak of Connemara". The final choice was a striking shot of Pádraic Bradley, a stylish *sean-nós* dancer of local fame and renown. The selection of a dancer as emblematic of *Pléaráca* reflects the central position of *sean-nós* dancing at an event such as this, which is a measure of its growth from a marginalised and neglected art form into a celebrated part of a conscious cultural tradition.

The *sean-nós* dancing competition is one of the highlights of *Pléaráca*, with hundreds crowding into *An Chistin*, the pub where it is held in An Cheathrú Rua. Donncha Ó hÉallaithe again: "*Sean-nós* dancing will get people here on a kind of 'communal high'. It creates this extraordinary energy. A step dancer in the *damhsa foghlamtha* style will not do this in Connemara. They may do in other areas but not here. It doesn't excite the same sort of reaction as *sean-nós* dancing does."

The extent of the audience reaction is apparent to many of the younger dancers who are lately crossing over from the *damhsa foghlamtha* style. Amongst these is a young girl called Róisín Ní Mhainnín of Rosmuc, whose dancing is much admired. A seasoned observer, Máirtín Jaimsie says of her: "*Tuigeann sí gur maith leis na daoine an sean-nós agus gur fearr an bualadh bos a fhaigheann sí nuair a dheineann sí píosa beag ar an sean-nós. Leagann sí an teach.*" ("She knows the people like the *sean-nós* and that she gets better applause when she dances it. She brings the house down.")

Róisín Ní Mhainnín is unusual as a dancer in that she successfully straddles the two contrasting worlds of dance which are found in the Galway region. Of all the criticisms levelled by Connemara dancers at the *Coimisiún* or *damhsa foghlamtha* style, the most cogent is that it is *mapáilte* (mapped out). The *damhsa foghlamtha* dancer is expected to reproduce exactly in performance the movement patterns and step elements as transmitted by the instructor. The notion of improvisation simply does not arise, and any innovation in terms of dance forms and repertoire is relayed via the dance teacher.

---

5   Donncha Ó hÉallaithe. Personal communication.

In contrast, the emphasis in the *sean-nós* style is on individuality, freedom of expression and personal creativity. *Tá a stíl féin ag chuile dhuine.* (Everyone has their own style.) There is a general perception that dance style and personality are intimately linked. Restrained, flamboyant, comic, wild, elegant, exhibitionistic – all these terms and more reflect the variety of dance styles in the *sean-nós*. A renowned dancer, Máirtín Beag Ó Gríofa, was described to me as having a style *"cosúil le bheith ag siúl ar uibheacha"* ("like walking on eggs"). Sometimes he would hold out his arms to the side as he danced. *"Shílfeá gur ag siúl ar rópa a bhí sé."* ("You'd think he was walking on a tight-rope.") "There was a very slight movement of his body with great concentration on footwork – minimalist footwork, but at the same time there was great power in it." Máirtín's son, Noel Ó Gríofa, is, in turn, a dancer of renown, having won the *Pléaráca* competition twice in four years. His style, however, is unlike his father's, being more extrovert and unrestrained.

A dancer with a particularly flamboyant style is Séamus Ó Duibheanaigh (Séamus Devanney) of Rosmuc. A big man, with a personality to match his frame, he speaks his self-confidence through the language of the dance. He capers, he stamps, his heels click, he bends, he advances and retires, his arms swing loose, now by his side, now shoulder high. In a final climactic gesture he leaps in the air, his arms over his head like a champion boxer who has just demolished his opponent. His dance sounds a challenge. Its echoes are primeval. Not all male dancers in the *sean-nós* style project this level or this type of force and power, though in all cases the dancer is involved in a form of display. One dancer described it as, *"ar nós coileach ag taispeáint don chearc go bhfuil sé beo"* ("like a cock showing the hen what life he has in him").

A champion dancer with a style very different from Séamus Ó Duibheanaigh's is Cóilín Dharach Seoighe of Rosmuc. He has won the *Pléaráca* trophy for adult *sean-nós* dancing several times. His style of dance is calm and controlled. His foot movements are precise and elegant. His body movement is minimal, with occasional slight swaying movement from left to right. His arms hang loosely by his sides but are never raised. The effect is of energy controlled and restrained. It is the body language of a man who does not need to raise his voice in order to be heard.

A young dancer with his own individual style is Seosamh Ó Neachtain of Spiddal, who is rising to prominence and is much in demand as a teacher of this style outside the *Gaeltacht*, a development which would have been inconceivable to the older generation of dancers.

Whereas male dancers at present outnumber females, the tradition has always included women dancers. Máirtín Jaimsie remarks of seeing women dancing in his young days (1950s), "*Ní raibh sé chomh fiáin ag na mná.*" ("Women dancers were not as wild [as the men].") Given that women at that period wore long heavy woollen skirts, it is likely that their dress would inevitably have restricted movement. This, combined with the prevalent social code demanding less demonstrative behaviour of women, at least in public, ensured a perceptible difference in male and female dance styles.

Today, this divergence is no longer applicable. Many young women dance with the same vigour as their male counterparts, though none, to date, has adopted the overtly exhibitionistic elements of a male dancer such as Séamus Ó Duibheanaigh. Of the many female dancers of recent years perhaps the most striking are Máire Ní Iarnáin of Carna and the already mentioned Róisín Ní Mhainnín of Rosmuc. Máire Ní Iarnáin, who died tragically in her mid-twenties, is best remembered for her historic victory in the 1988 *sean-nós* dance competition organised by *Telegael* (an Irish-language television production company, based in Connemara) – the first ever national television broadcast of this dance style.[6] Against very stiff competition – including Séamus Ó Méalóid of Ráth Cairn, Séamus Ó Duibheanaigh and Cóilín Seoighe – she was awarded first place after a display of dazzling virtuosity. Casually dressed in jumper, jeans and ankle boots, she combined grace and elegance with strength and self-assertion. From a famed musical family – her brothers are well-known players of flute and accordeon – she "got her dancing" from her mother, who encouraged her to hoist herself between two chairs so as to "get up off her body and allow her to concentrate on the steps".[7] This aerial training would seem to have been designed to produce a style which is highly prized in the *sean-nós*, where the dancer is *go deas*

---

6   *Telegael* video.
7   Donncha Ó hÉallaithe. Personal communication.

éadrom ar a chois (lovely and light on his feet). Again, Máire's choice of rubber-soled footwear would have contributed to this effect.

In contrast, the young dancer Róisín Ní Mhainnín selects hard-soled boots for her performance. Her style emphasises another aspect of the Connemara *sean-nós* tradition, what dancers call *timeáil*.[8] Its characteristic clicking sound is what has prompted some observers to liken this dance style to that of Andalusia in southern Spain. Máirtín Mac Donnacha is another noted exponent of the art of *timeáil*, and his dancing is much admired in Connemara.

Róisín Ní Mhainnín is perceived as a future champion in the *sean-nós* style. Her composure and self-confidence as a performer may owe something to her years of training in the *damhsa foghlamtha* style. Her adoption of the *sean-nós* and her ability to impose her own personality on the dance is seen by older dancers as a confirmation that the tradition lives on and yet is not stagnant. *Forbairt* (development) is seen generally as desirable. The current lack of codification of the stylistic elements of the form appears to be linked to a desire to avoid what are perceived as the excessively bureaucratic features of the *damhsa foghlamtha* organisation.

Any consideration of the notion of identity and *sean-nós* dance would be incomplete without a reference to the ideas of the film-maker Bob Quinn, who left the relatively comfortable world of RTÉ[9] in the 1970s to live and work in the Connemara *Gaeltacht*. He had first seen *sean-nós* dancing in 1964 while making a film in Connemara and was struck by its remoteness from any concept of Irish dancing previously experienced by him. The dancer was Stiofán Ó Cualáin of Carna, who is regarded as a major exponent of the style. As a film-maker, Quinn was primarily affected by the visual impact of movement, and Ó Cualáin's dancing created an indelible impression. The arms moving freely, the stamping, clicking feet, the body now swaying, now erect – all reminded him of the dance of southern Spain, the *flamenco*.

His excitement at his discovery of *sean-nós* dance, which seemed to him nothing short of exotic, led to thoughts of the history of trade, of sea

---

8 See appendix.
9 *Radio Teilifís Éireann*, the national television and radio network.

voyages, of political alliances, of musical links between Galway and the outside world. He was determined to explore the thesis that the west of Ireland was not a remote, insular, introverted region, but instead had been open to influences from Europe and from North Africa since the Middle Ages. In his film *Atlantean*, he presents evidence from the worlds of art, linguistics and music in a highly-individualistic and visually fascinating mélange.

The film opens with a shot of a *púcán* (a Galway hooker) – a sailing boat used to transport coastal cargo until the 1950s. A man is playing the accordeon on deck. One of the crew coils a rope and then . . . he begins to dance. Against the background of his graceful movements, with close-ups of his feet *ag timeáil* – the tapping movements which reminded Bob Quinn of *flamenco* – the commentary begins:

> He had traced the connection to Spain but he was stating the obvious because nobody disputed this connection. Even this Connemara dancing could be explained away as being related to *flamenco*. In Connemara it's called "the battering". There was the well-known religious affinity. Both Spain and Ireland were strongly Roman Catholic. Thousands of Irish priests were educated at Salamanca. Thousands of Irish soldiers went into exile in Spain. But it was an historical cul-de-sac for if everything could be traced to Spain, there wasn't much point in searching further. But he wasn't satisfied. Now isn't that strange? We are happy to admit Catholic Spain's influence, but Islamic North Africa, only a few miles further, might not exist as far as we're concerned. Could it have something to do with old religious rivalries? It was time to start bridging that gap.[10]

Bob Quinn's odyssey to the shores of North Africa may not provide incontrovertible evidence for his theories of Arab influence in the Irish "western world", but it is without doubt that his vision of Connemara as being somehow touched by the rays of an Andalusian sun is appealing to a people living among grey rocks under a grey sky. The famed Stiofán Ó Cualáin, Bob Quinn's first contact with *sean-nós* dance, recently referred to the link with *flamenco* during his adjudication of the *Telegael sean-nós*

---

10   From the sound-track of *Atlantean*.

competition which indicates the extent to which this exotic idea has become part of the dance identity of Connemara.

As we have seen, competitiveness has always been part of the vernacular culture. In the Connemara *Gaeltacht*, rivalry between dancers might develop spontaneously during a *babhla rince* (a bout of dance). "Sometimes people would face up each other and dance against each other. There'd be an element of a kind of challenge involved in that."[11]

Although well-known dancers will still be called on to perform during a night out in a pub or at a social function, whether public or private, it is undoubtedly the case that the main dance arena is now the *comórtas damhsa ar an sean-nós*. For better or for worse, the predominance of the challenge aspect of traditional dance practice will inevitably shape the form and content of the dance in the Connemara region.

Some reservations are expressed concerning the effect of organised competitions, particularly where, as in Connemara, they have come to be the main arena for dancers' performance. For instance, fears are expressed concerning the possibility that participants might alter their style to suit the perceived requirements of an adjudicator. One observer remarked: "In a desire to win, dancers might go beyond the natural development of the art form that is *sean-nós* and there would become two styles of *sean-nós* dancing – one for competition and one for the rest of us."[12] Similarly, traditional musicians express concern at the basis of the annual music competitions held by *Comhaltas Ceoltóirí Éireann* (the Council of Irish Musicians) which culminate in the finals at *Fleadh Cheoil na hÉireann* each year. Paddy Glackin, the well-known traditional fiddler and RTÉ (radio) producer, said recently:

> Competitions, in some ways, can bring on a certain standard; but what standard? How often have we heard very good regional players going up in competition and not getting a look-in, getting adjudicated by people who know nothing about it; and as a result, I believe that competitions in many ways have contributed to the demise of regional styles of playing in some cases. I mean, how can you adjudicate between people like Denis Murphy

---

11   Donncha Ó hEallaithe. Personal communication.
12   *Ibid.*

and John Doherty, two wonderful players from different parts of the country with their own way of expressing music? How any one individual man can get up and say that this particular man is better than the other![13]

The question of adjudication of *sean-nós* dance is a thorny one. The adjudicator should know the style intimately; thus, will most likely be local. Being local, s/he will be unhappy at the idea, or possibly the social consequences, of selecting one dancer for honour and thereby slighting others. Many dancers express extreme reluctance, if not total opposition, to the idea of judging their peers. The solution can sometimes be to import an "outsider" who at least can escape from the inevitable choreographical post-mortem. However, by the same token, the perceived impartiality of this "outside" judge may pose another problem, the likelihood that s/he will not be entirely *au fait* with the *sean-nós* form and may thus apply inappropriate aesthetic considerations in deciding a winner. I was talking recently to an elderly *Coimisiún* adjudicator, and she told me what happened when she went to adjudicate a *sean-nós* dancing competition in Connemara in the 1960s:

> I thought I was going to the usual dancing-school thing . . . The next thing was, four or five great big fellas got up on the stage and they started with this awful thing – they all did the same thing and I don't know what in the name of Providence what they were doing . . . so . . . I gave the prize to the fella that had the most children! They came over to tell me all the children they had and the fella with the most children got the prize![14]

Technical considerations aside, the business of the *sean-nós* competition is taken very seriously. Each dancer in a competition such as that held during Pléaráca Chonamara carries the hopes not alone of family and friends but also of his/her locality. This, together with the high status accorded the winner and the prize of a handsome trophy, means that rivalry is extremely keen. The organisers are aware of the more unpleasant overtones associated with the usual notion of competition and have included

---

13   Peter McNamee, ed., *Traditional Music: Whose Music?* (Belfast: The Institute of Irish Studies, Queen University of Belfast, 1991), p. 36.

14   From an interview with an informant who wishes not to be identified here.

an award for the most "humorous" dancer among the prizes. The participation of clowning and grotesque dancers, often involving a parody of the
sean-nós style itself, serves to defuse the tension arising from the more
serious aspect of the night's business. Despite occasional murmurings at
the juxtaposition of real dancing and what is seen by some as a gross
mockery of the tradition, the comic dancing remains, by popular acclaim,
an integral part of an event which has above all been designed as a
celebration of the solo *sean-nós* dance style in all its diversity.

The future shape of *sean-nós* dance is subject to many variables. The
basic elements of the tradition might possibly be enriched by innovation.
Far from fearing influences from without, the local attitude would seem to
be that the tradition is strong enough to successfully adapt to and incorporate new dance ideas. As one dancer put it to me, "*Is féidir céimeannaí a
ghoid ó aon damhsóir sa domhan.*" ("Steps can be stolen from any dancer in the
world.") In recent times the dance style of Connemara has moved centre
stage and has almost achieved the status accorded to the *sean-nós* singing
tradition. From being a neglected and marginalised art, it has become a
badge of local identity which ensures its central position in the unique
culture of the Connemara *Gaeltacht*.

Chapter Ten

Last Words

U NTIL RECENTLY, THE popular image of Irish dance was a stage performance by young girls in white knee socks, short dresses bespattered with the *Book of Kells* and crowned with what we used to call sausage ringlets. The heavily embroidered and occasionally lurid colour schemes of the modern dance schools[1] have no basis in historic Irish dress and serve simply to identify and advertise the school concerned. The main item of the boys' stage and competition dress, the kilt (which is sometimes teamed with an embroidered cummerbund and velvet waistcoat), is the source of much painful mockery of young male dancers and is often cited as the main reason why so many boys abandon competition-style Irish dancing before their teenage years. Specialised shoes are also worn. These consist of either a soft leather, laced pump or Brigadoon for light dancing or a specially engineered leather shoe for heavy dancing (hornpipe, double jig, etc.), often featuring built-up toes and synthetic heels with, at one stage, bubble protrusions to assist in the production of the desired clicking sound effects.

---

1   For details of the history of Irish dance costumes, see Dr John Cullinane, *Irish Dancing Costumes* (Cork: published by the author, 1996); and Martha Robb, *Irish Dancing Costume* (Dublin: Country House, 1998).

Whereas the competitive spirit of the traditional dancer arose spontaneously at a social gathering, the modern schools concentrate on producing dancers who will enter and hopefully score well in competitions. Both the traditional and modern styles are made up of the same basic stepping elements, but the difference lies in the mode of execution of these movements, the body posture of the dancer and the tempo of the accompanying music. One of the features of the modern dancing school style is a pronounced and often very rapid movement forward, back or diagonally, as well as a tendency to spring up and down during the execution of a step. The use of very high knee movements such as in the modern side step of the reel are said to date from the 1950s. The late Tony McNulty from Gormanstown, County Meath, says that this movement was called the Belfast hop and signalled the opening of the floodgates of change involving high leaping and "dancing across the beat" (syncopation).[2] The noted Dundalk fiddle-player, Mrs Rose O'Connor, who is a veteran of playing for dancing-school competitions, describes the high-kicking movements of the modern dancers as wag-o'-the-wall dancing, as they remind her of the movements of a clock's pendulum swinging to and fro.

The skill required in the modern dancing-school style is not in question. Indeed, their dancers' proficiency is truly wondrous. Their repertoire is still based on the traditional dances, but many observers would maintain that their dance style is moving further and further away from its source: the old-style southern traditional dance techniques as exemplified by dancers such as Joe O'Donovan from Cork or James Keane from Labasheeda, County Clare.

Joe O'Donovan is an expert dancer in the highly developed Cork style which has been so influential in the field of traditional dance in Ireland generally. He has also put pen to paper on the topic of the dancing tradition which, he feels, has suffered considerably in recent times. In his view, "a substantial part of Irish dancing is so far removed from the traditional form that it can no longer be said to be traditional. Tourists and others watching some of these dances may well believe they are watching traditional dancing and

---

2   Tony McNulty, Gormanstown, Co. Meath, 1998, coll. Seán Corcoran, ITMA SCDAT53.

it would be hard to blame them for this for indeed many of the dancers have the same impression."[3]

The changes in dance style brought about by the modern dancing-schools are detailed:

> The old-style "close to the floor" solo dancing is replaced by high stepping and heel clicking which is more akin to acrobatic and ballet dancing than to Irish dancing. Economy of space and accuracy of movement with simple steps has given way to an extravagant use of space with intricate movements so much so that the music, particularly the hornpipe, has been slowed down so much to accommodate the intricacies and extra taps, that the traditional musician is no longer happy to play for modern dancers.[4]

This view is echoed by Muiris Ó Rócháin, director of the Willie Clancy Summer School and a well-known and respected figure in traditional music circles in Ireland: "Musicians will say that the music for these dances is non-creative and restricted to a small set of tunes which are [in turn] restricted to the bare essentials. There is no spontaneity and no opportunity for a musician to develop."[5]

The modern dancer who is dancing to competition standard will use steps with a highly ornate sound pattern involving syncopation and a multiplicity of trebling movements which require music at a speed referred to as "strict tempo" by the directors of the dancing schools. The late Tony McNulty, who trained as a dancer in the 1940s, says that "hornpipes are now at a snail's pace to put in lots of double trebles".[6] This extremely ornamented style in which the impulse seems to be to, as it were, defy the time signature and over-embellish each bar of the music in order to impress an adjudicator has become an embarrassment to An Coimisiún le Rincí Gaelacha, the governing body of the modern dancing schools. Lately, the Coimisiún has instructed the dancing schools to alter the speed of the music used by its dancers so as to restore it somewhat to the original faster traditional speed.

---

3   Joe O' Donovan, *Traditional Dancing Today* (1983, unpublished).
4   *Ibid*.
5   *The Irishman* , San Francisco, June 1983.
6   Tony McNulty, 1998, coll. Seán Corcoran, I.T.M.A., SCDAT53.

Another area which distinguishes the modern dancing school style from the traditional style is the element of standardisation which the dance schools have imposed. Consequently, a national and indeed latterly an international audience has been conditioned to perceive an extreme modification and "heightening" of the Munster style as "real" Irish dancing. As Muiris Ó Rócháin says: "Competitions organised by the Gaelic League for dancing disqualified very accomplished dancers because they did not conform to the regularity of the types of steps which the Gaelic League had set up."[7]

The *raison d'être* of the modern dance schools is competition, and pupils are expected to dedicate themselves to taking part in the bewildering array of gradings appropriate to their level of performance. Boys generally drop out of dancing classes at puberty, often as a response to peer pressure which sees Irish dancing as "sissy". Girls continue to dance into their late teens, after which their competition days are over. The only avenue towards a career in Irish dance has been, until recently, as an accredited teacher. In Ireland, this generally provided a meagre enough living. However, the growing interest abroad amongst the Irish diaspora in the United States, Britain, Australia, Canada and New Zealand, indeed "wherever green is worn", has meant that the market for Irish dance teaching is growing apace and the financial rewards can be considerable.[8] Through the weight of sheer numbers as well as an emphasis on innovation based largely on borrowings from stage dance, the American influence on the world of competition-style Irish dance reached an all-time high in the 1980s.

Two of the dancers who achieved fame in the American-Irish dance world were Michael Flatley and Jean Butler. Both had danced on stage with Irish music groups such as the Chieftains and received a warm reception, but nothing could have prepared them for the overwhelming fame which was to follow their appearance in an interval act during the 1994 Eurovision Song Contest. Irish dance had long been a feature of the American music-hall scene, where even legendary musicians of the early 1900s such as the fiddlers James Morrison and Michael Coleman would dance a "tidy

---

7   *The Irishman* , San Francisco, June 1983.
8   Annie May Fahy, my dancing teacher, says, "It's only the penguins in the Antarctic that aren't doing Irish dancing nowadays."

clog" as part of their stage act. As we have seen, Irish dancing on stage had largely come to mean a stiff-backed performance by a troupe of young dancers wearing the regulation dance dresses rigid with embroidery. An honourable exception to this is the *Siamsa Tíre* show in Tralee, County Kerry, which has incorporated steps from the older traditional dancers in the area into its repertoire.

Yet here in the 1990s, in the unlikely setting of the Euro-extravaganza, appeared a totally new dance phenomenon produced by RTÉ's Moya Doherty. It featured a veritable chorus line of attractive young women with long flowing hair, clad in short velvety dresses and partnered by young men in fashionably cut black trousers and flowing shirts, who provided the choreographical accompaniment to the leading pair who danced a love duet, Irish style. The familiar batters, shuffles, drums, rocks and cuts were all there; the dancers wore the specially engineered black footwear which had hitherto seemed so unglamorous. But this was Irish dance as it had never been seen before: an unashamedly spectacular display which, for once, accepted the sexual undertones of the dance and revelled in its power. The sound was magnified to a volcanic rumble by the combined power of the dancers' feet. The accompanying music by Bill Whelan had Irish overtones but was obviously newly composed. Its rhythms underlay the thunderous footwork of Flatley and the balletic movements of Jean Butler. The result was electrifying. Ireland was agog. The familiar had been utterly transformed. *Riverdance* was in spate. Its power could turn a generating station, let alone a mill. In the years since 1994, the *Riverdance* show has become the single most successful production using Irish dance as its centrepiece. Acres of print have been produced, analysing and commenting on the *Riverdance* phenomenon, most of them eulogising its achievements, although occasionally a dissenting view has bubbled to the surface.

Currently, the commercial success of *Riverdance* continues unabated with three separate troupes under the names "Lee", "Liffey" and "Lagan" (the names of Irish rivers) touring the world to continued acclaim.

With Michael Flatley's break from *Riverdance* came yet another large-scale stage presentation using the vehicle of Irish dance. Flatley's *Lord of the Dance* was created as a showcase for his particular tap-influenced style. The costumes and settings were pure vaudeville. The theme of the golden-haired hero overcoming the forces of darkness was hardly new, but as a commercial venture it was spectacularly successful. Amongst the gaggles of little girls and their mothers who form the mainstay of the Flatley fan base, he has achieved veritable pin-up status. The former much-resented image of the Irish male dancer as a sissy in a skirt has been replaced by the iconography of black-leather-sheathed thighs and oiled pectorals. The scale of the commercial success of *Riverdance* and *Lord of the Dance* is unprecedented. Irish dance is now synonymous with glamour and is a passport to world fame. This lesson is not lost on the legions of young Irish dancers and their families. Between *Riverdance* and the newer *Feet of Flames* and *Spirit of the Dance*, there are almost 200 positions for professional dancers who have been trained by the Irish dancing schools.

This is seen as a welcome development by the dance teachers generally, although some are rather rueful that their hard work is not always acknowledged. One such teacher said: "The dancers are very appreciative of the training they have received but it seems that generally the teachers are a forgotten part of the equation." A prominent member of the Irish Dance Commission expressed a similar view when he remarked that the *Riverdance* and other shows had benefited from the training provided by its schools, whereas the financial rewards were directed elsewhere.

After *Riverdance* and *Lord of the Dance*, registrations in Irish dancing schools more than doubled. One teacher talked of the problem of convincing enthusiastic parents that their four-year-old daughter could not be expected to perform *Riverdance*-style steps after two lessons. Indeed, the pressure on young dancers produced by the competitions at the *feiseanna* is a constant factor in a young dancer's life. A mother felt moved to write in the letters column of the magazine *Irish Dancing* of January 1999 that, in her opinion:

> The constant practising and extreme stress of the *Feis* can sometimes be too much for the dancers who are after all only kids. There are times when a bit of fun is needed to lighten the load, something which some of the teachers and parents I have met seem to have forgotten. I have seen many children

in tears, or, worse still, looking across to teacher or parent with sheer terror in their eyes after making a simple mistake.

An important feature of the dancing school world is the element of expense involved in kitting out a dancer. One of the spin-offs of the success of the large-scale dance shows has been the emergence of a veritable industry centred entirely around the world of the dancing school pupil. A prominent teacher, perforce anonymous, remarks: "It puts teachers under a lot of pressure because we are aware of how much money has been spent on a child. Parents want their child to look good but I cringe when I think of the amount that can be spent."

A modern state-of-the-art dress can cost anything from £400 to £800. Then you have the specialised shoes, the embroidered tiaras, plaited hair bands, satin pants, dress covers, half-covers, smocks, aprons, magic wand curlers, caps and Kangol berets to go over the hair curlers, Tara brooches, "poodle" socks, "banana clip" hair pieces, headbands, crowns, scrunchies and finally, wigs.

Wigs are, undoubtedly, a big talking point in the Irish dance world. Melanie Gammage, a purveyor of dance accessories throughout the UK and Ireland, tells us:

> Wigs can be a great boon – but you have to "work" the wig – to make it look and feel natural. Each wig comes with a hair net and you must store it in the net to avoid "frizz". Our wigs are made from synthetic hair and pieces start at around £50. It can take about 50 hair grips to secure a wig properly and the dancer must feel absolutely confident before taking to the stage. Once you have the wig on, you should treat it like real hair, working with it to make it right for you.

Melanie advises against the use of wigs for young children. "If they have long, good hair they should curl it. It's good for them to understand the effort made to look right for the dance. However, if children of any age are doing an evening demonstration and, say, going straight from school, then a wig is a terrific help."

The hair issue has produced a degree of controversy – a form of choreographical "wigs on the green". Under the byline "Sounding Off", in the

January 1999 issue of *Irish Dancing*, an observer of the 1998 Great Britain Irish Dancing Championships writes:

> The sheer gaudiness everywhere of lovely children festooned with WIGS subsumes all else. Not even the most delicate cut or entrechat can provide sufficient antidote to this spectacle. Some of these Dolly Parton wigs are half the physical size of the dancer. They are a gross embarrassment to Irish dancing . . . Mass wigging of dancers is a recent phenomenon but it is a malaise that has been taunting us for years in the more real sense of the children's own hair being tortured for hours on end. There is no other recreation that I am aware of where children can be found kneeling face down in their bed the night before a competition because of hair curlers making it too uncomfortable to put one's head on the pillow.

The rationale behind the obsessive pursuit of a head of curls and the recent tendency towards wigging is that dancers are judged on their "lift", especially in the "light" dances. It is considered worthwhile for dancers to endure the discomfort involved, in order to create the illusion of natural muscular lift produced by the effect of the artificial bounce of a head of tightly curled long hair.

As before with the "Tiara controversy", which resulted in the elimination by the *Coimisiún* of excessively bejewelled headgear imported via the American-Irish dancing schools, coupled with the furore over the excessive, pistol-sharp clicking sound produced by the transatlantic "bubble" heels and the recent legislation surrounding the length of dancers' dresses *à la Riverdance*, it seems likely that the governing body of Irish dance will move to intervene on the "wig issue", which threatens to become an embarrassment on the Irish dancing scene.

The world of the Irish dancing schools is largely the preserve of children and most adults' experience of Irish dance is through the medium of the commercial dance-shows where their role is as consumers, as passive observers. This contrasts very much with the other main dance event of the recent past, namely, the revival of set dancing. The set-dance revival warrants a book in itself and its history has already been traced in various publications. Its main organ is the magazine *The Set Dancer*, which has become a vehicle for the views of the prime movers in the revival.

The sets had been danced continuously in small pockets, mainly in the south-west of Ireland, into modern times and, aided by the promotion of set-dancing competitions run by the GAA and *Comhaltas Ceoltóirí Éireann* in the 1960s, they were beginning to generate interest amongst a new generation of dancers. Many of the older dancers who had previously danced the sets purely for enjoyment were saddened by the divisive effect of competitive dancing. Martin Byrnes of Quin, County Clare, a noted set dancer, said of the new style: "Dance teachers added new pieces for competitions. The audience and outside adjudicators would be highly impressed with the gimmicks but they didn't know it was not traditional. Competitions destroyed it and are still destroying it."[9] An emphasis on regimentation – involving costume, body posture and footwork – became the hallmark of these competitions, reaching absurd heights on occasion as when points were allocated according to the ability of the dancers to march on stage in semi-military formation. This distortion of the normal practice of the dance has echoes in the modern dancing school competition ethic which has resulted in an extremely rigid code of theory and practice. In this regard, it is noteworthy that most of the adjudicators in these early set-dancing competitions came from the modern dancing school world and were, in many cases, totally unaware of the very existence of an "untamed" Irish dance tradition.

One of the key elements in the tremendous success of the set-dancing movement was, undoubtedly, the presence of a generation who had grown up during the Irish music renaissance of the 1960s and '70s and had experienced the music as merely passive listeners to a performance, whether in an informal "session" or in a concert-style setting. The excitement generated by the realisation that this was *dance* music and that, furthermore, there existed a body of dance outside the more rigid confines of the average *céilí* produced a cultural chain reaction. The hitherto relatively inert audience for the music, whose percussive participation had been confined to foot tapping, coin clicking, hand clapping and bottle clinking, saw an amazing vista opening up. They could, for the first time, really participate in the world of Irish music, even if they didn't aspire to play a note.

---

9   Larry Lynch, *Set Dances of Ireland. Tradition and Evolution* (Miltown Malbay, County, Clare: Séadna Books, in collaboration with Dal gCais Publications, 1989), p. 18.

The initiation of classes in set dancing at the 1982 Willie Clancy Summer School in Miltown Malbay, County Clare, was, more that anything else, the spark that lit the revival's fuse. Within months, classes were being held all over the country in cities, towns and villages. In Dublin, in the headquarters of Na Píobairí Uilleann (the Uilleann Pipers' organisation), a group calling itself Brook's Academy began to invite dancers from around the country to teach their local sets, whether revived from memory or still currently danced socially. Due to the demand for set-dancing "workshops" and weekends, set-dancing teachers had to familiarise themselves with an ever-growing repertoire.

Soon, set dancers were boasting that they knew ten or twelve sets. This was in contrast to the pre-revival situation, when local people knew one or at most two sets and really danced them, as opposed to simply knowing the figures. In other words, they knew the set so well that they could relax into it and put in all the little subtleties of tipping, tapping, stamping, gliding or battering – in short, the touches that gave the dance its unique local flavour. Learning a set in isolation without ever having seen the real thing meant that a lot of new set-dance enthusiasts missed out on the natural learning process in the tradition, whereby youngsters absorbed the dance by a sort of cultural osmosis and could look to skilled dancers in their locality for inspiration, guidance and encouragement. In this context, I once heard a neophyte set dancer in County Louth dismiss the Caledonian set as "boring" because it was "all the same thing". This girl had never had the opportunity of seeing Clare set dancers in action, and I felt at the time that even if she *had* witnessed the likes of Ollie and Marie Conway, Willie Keane, Michael Currucane or Martie Malley in full flight, she would probably have been unable to detect what their feet were doing, let alone imitate it. Maybe, since then, she has visited Clare and discovered the magic for herself.

Speaking of Clare and learner dancers, I still remember cringing as I watched a loud-mouthed American, who had just had his first lessons in the Caledonian, pushing and pulling the dancers in Gleeson's pub in Coor, County Clare, where they dance a unique form of this set which allows a whole floorful of dancers to participate instead of the usual four couples. "Two opposite two! Two opposite two!" he bellowed, oblivious not only to his offence to good manners but also to the fact that he was instructing some of the best traditional dancers that ever stood on a dance floor. I afterwards had a quiet word in his ear, but that's another story.

At the burgeoning set-dance classes in the early 1980s, the plain, the Sliabh Luachra, the Connemara, the mazurka and the lancers sets followed hard on one another's heels. Manuals of set dances were produced and collecting trips were organised to talk to older dancers and piece together sets which had fallen into disuse. Totally new dances were also created, such as the Piper's set, composed by Terry Moylan of Dublin. Set-dancing workshops became a feature of the dancing scene nationwide, and the pressure was on to provide ever more and more obscure and "recently discovered" sets in order to satisfy the demands of the throngs of dancers who flocked into the classes. The enthusiasm of these newcomers to the Irish dance scene was infectious. Commentators such as Michael Tubridy, who had been part of a Clare "exile's" music and dance club in Dublin in the early 1960s, were amazed and delighted to see the old plain set, which had died out in Clare, being revived by Connie Ryan in the 1980s. However, as set followed set in a plethora of workshops and weekends of instruction, it became apparent that the numbers game mentality of some learners was alarming many set-dance instructors who were aware of the subtleties involved in traditional dancing. Tony Brogan, who began dancing sets in 1962, well before the frenzy of the revival says:

> I do not want to appear to be a wet blanket or a spoil sport – we all dance sets for enjoyment – but if the lovely subtle variations that distinguish one set from another are not to be lost irretrievably something needs to be done before it is too late. I say this because I have heard people say that they know up to forty sets but when they go up dancing one notes that all they know is that the first figure is pass through, the second is . . . etc. Do they know the difference in footwork between one locality and another? They dance but one step. Do they know whether ladies chain high or low; hand, forearm or elbow? Do they know if the set, traditionally, was danced softly or with vigour; sedately or with gusto?

> Divil a bit, but they know 37 sets.

Some set-dance teachers tried to give their pupils a taste of the real thing by bringing them to localities where the set was still danced traditionally. Given the attitude of some of the revival dancers involving a sort of dance-menu mind set, having them relate to real dancers who knew their own local set intimately and simply danced it threw up some interesting scenarios. Terry Moylan recounts a visit to Dan O'Connell's pub in Knocknagree on the Cork/Kerry border with some of his pupils from Brook's Academy in Dublin. He was sure that they would be bowled over by their experience of the night's dance fun as he himself had been on his first visit some years previously. In the course of the evening, one of his learners came up to him to complain, aghast at the idea of there being only two dances on the night's "programme" – the polka set and the waltz. Terry says: "It just had never occurred to me that anyone would find this inadequate. If you go to a chateau to buy wine, you know that what you are drinking has come straight up out of the ground around you, and you don't expect them to provide a wine list representing other regions."

This rather sobering experience and other similar encounters seemed to indicate that the set-dancing revival was attracting some newcomers to dancing who had little or no previous connection with the world of Irish music and were attracted to set dancing as they would be to any other leisure pursuit. This has resulted in a growing number of dancers who, according to Mick Mulkerrin, the dancer and teacher, "don't seem to understand the music, or dance the dances as they should be danced, or as they would have been danced". Mick has used his skills as a step dancer to attempt to instil into the revival set dancers an awareness of the need to *dance* a set as opposed to merely knowing the figures: He counsels that step elements such as battering should be used sparingly and adds ruefully: "The message doesn't seem to be getting through, or the enthusiasm for dancing, the adrenalin rush, the addiction, outweigh any respect for the finer points of tradition." The comparison which is sometimes made between physical activities such as marathon running and set dancing is not lost on observers of the scene who have recently noticed dancers turning up at a workshop or function with sweat bands, two fresh towels and extra tee-shirts as if for a workout. Frank Hall, an American anthropologist who participated joyously in the early days of the set dance revival in Ireland, has lately seen signs of what he calls "the dreaded, vexed and possibly inescapable aerobic/performance shift".

The fact that so many seasoned members of the set dance movement are expressing certain reservations about aspects of the revival is an indication that the headlong rush of enthusiasm of the "new wave" of dancers is not likely to overwhelm the living tradition. At present, there are over seventy set-dancing classes running weekly, as well as countless workshop weekends and literally hundreds of *céilís* and "set sessions". There have never been so many people dancing in Ireland; never so many experiencing the "joy of sets".

Meanwhile, quietly, they are dancing Highlands and polkas in Garrison and in Lahey; they're doing the brush dance on Sunday mornings in Carberry's of the Back Strand in Drogheda; Johnny Smith is cutting a caper in the Jolly Old Cross in Cormeen; Ted McGowan is urging the dancers to take the floor in the Róisín Dubh in Gurteen; and in *Réalt na Maidne* in An Cheathrú Rua, they're *ag jiveáil agus ag válsáil* to the melodious tones of John Beag and his guitar. That's the story – the story without end. *"Faoi do chois!"* 10

---

10 In London in 1969, a satirical news-sheet called *"Focailín"* (a wee word) made a brief but glorious appearance. One issue carried a special offer – a "Teach yourself Irish Percussion Kit". This included a set of white plastic spoons for silent practice in the privacy of your own home. The accompanying booklet was entitled – A *Beginner's Guide to Irish traditional music. Is it a jig or a reel? – the mystery unravelled.*

Appendix

Stepping

Since many readers will have little or no idea what exactly is happening during the flurry of movement that goes into a "step", here are some of the step elements in traditional step dance, together with a brief descriptions of how they are done. Based on observation of dancers throughout Ireland over the last twenty years or more, they form the beginning of a process of unravelling the complexity of the various styles found in the country. As this appendix is intended for the general reader, they are somewhat abbreviated. Also, the use of terms such as "southern", "western" and "northern" styles will, undoubtedly, be refined in the future as the study of Irish step dance is further developed.

The Southern or Munster Style

Since standardisation has as yet not affected the living tradition, it must be understood that not all dancers in the Munster style will make use of all these step-elements. Some dancers will not have names for the elements they use, and, most confusingly, different names may be used in different parts of the region for the same movement. Munster stepping may also be seen in many other parts of the country since it was the only style to have been codified and systematically taught.

It forms the basis of the style used by the modern Irish dancing schools, albeit in a "heightened", or as they describe it, a "developed" form. It also is the origin of the stepping to be seen in *Riverdance* and other stage shows, since the choreographers and dancers in these shows are the product of the modern dancing schools.

The most prominent feature of the southern style is that the dancer is poised on the ball of the foot. The foot does not drop on to the heel except on rare occasions. The basic foot position is feet side by side with toes pointed outwards, but not exaggeratedly so.

Single Shuffle

This can be performed in place but usually involves a forward movement. It has been described by some dancing teachers as "kicking a small pebble". Begin with basic position and move forward, striking the floor a glancing blow lightly with the ball of the right foot thrown forward and then lightly stepping on the same foot. Repeat off the left foot. The southern hornpipe makes use of the single shuffle in many steps, particularly in the lead or introductory step. In the hornpipe, the single shuffle directly mirrors the rhythm of the music.

Double Shuffle

From basic position, step on to left foot, then throw the right foot forward, striking the floor with the ball of the foot and immediately return it to the starting position, striking the floor again on the way back. Thus the floor is struck three times, and these strokes correspond with the three quavers forming half of a bar in a double jig. The name comes from the double stroke given by the foot that is thrown forward. A typical bar in double jig time would make use of two double shuffles.

Treble Shuffle

Begin, as in the double shuffle, with the feet side by side. Step on to the left foot, then kick the right foot forward, back and forward again, striking the floor with the ball of the foot during each movement.

Appendix

The Heel Plant

The dancing foot is swung forward and the floor is struck by the rear edge of the heel, with toes turned up.

The Heel Kick: Inside and Outside

The inside edge of the heel of the leading (dancing) foot is kicked a glancing forward blow by the inside toe of the other foot. In the old-style Munster jig, the kick is directed at the outside of the opposite heel.

The Cut

There are three types: the ground cut, the half cut and the full cut. This step element basically involves crossing one foot over the other.

The ground cut: the dancing foot moves forward across and in front of the other foot and touches the floor once before returning to the starting position.

The half cut: the dancing foot crosses the other foot in a low aerial position just over the opposite instep before returning to position.

The full cut: the dancing foot is swung inwardly, heel first, across and in front of the other foot, rising to a position halfway between the knee and the ankle before returning to position. Traditionally this step element has been used mainly in reel dancing but it also figures prominently in the old moneen jigs, and single and hop jigs.

The Rock or Puzzle

The dancing foot is crossed and firmly gripped behind the other foot with both feet positioned on the ball of the foot and facing forwards. The feet are "locked" at ankle level; and in this position they bend ("rock") from side to side at the ankles, with the body weight shifting as required. Sometimes the dancing foot may cross in front of the other foot (forward rock). Usually three rocks are made during a step.

The Drum

There are three types of drum: the single the double and the treble.

In the single drum, in this case the right drum, the dancer steps on to the left foot, the right foot is simultaneously raised. The drumming sound which gives this movement its name is produced by striking the floor first with the right toe and then the right heel. The full movement takes up three quavers or half a bar in jig time.

The double drum is a simple repetition of this movement on the same dancing foot, and the treble drum is a repetition three times.

The *Sean Nós* Dance Style of Connemara

As indicated in the main text, the Connemara *sean-nós* style differs from the Munster style in that it does not involve the process of teaching the dance in a formal master/mistress – pupil setting. Dancers in this tradition are at pains to distance themselves from the "learnt" styles of dance taught in the modern dancing schools which they see as *mapáilte* or "mapped out". In the Connemara style the dancer will string together a series of movement patterns to form an eight-bar step. The foot position is more as in normal walking in that the dancer is not primarily positioned on the balls of the feet as in the Munster style. The movement known as *timeáil* ("timing") which is a prominent feature of this style involves a form of heel-and-toe stepping which links it with the other main "non-dancing master" style, which is described here as the northern style. Finally, and most importantly, each eight-bar step is *not* doubled, i.e. is *not* repeated on the left foot.

The distinctive *timeáil* movement in this style is performed thus:

Each count takes 1 quaver. Start with feet together, side by side, heels *slightly* raised.

Count

1	Strike the tip of the right heel on the floor.
2	Step down on to ball of right foot.
3	Strike the tip of the left heel on the floor.
4	Step down on to ball of the left foot.

The balance of the body shifts from the ball of one foot to the other. On count 1, it is on the ball of the left foot; on count 2 it moves back to the right, then back to the left on count 4.

Finish

Often a step, which takes up eight bars of the reel, will be made up of a series of *movement patterns* taking up six bars, ending with a *finish* which takes up two bars. A typical finish is a backwards movement thus:

Count

1–4	Step back on right foot so that toe of right foot is positioned just in line with heel of left foot.
5–8	Step back on left foot so that toe of left foot is positioned just in line with heel of right foot.

REPEAT

In stepping back there is a slight bounce on the foot supporting the body weight (left in count 1, right in count 5), so that the whole movement is not flat-footed.

Steps

Some steps are danced more or less "in place" for six bars followed by a two-bar finish.

An example is this simple but attractive element which is danced first off the right foot, then repeated in mirror image off the left foot. This movement takes up two bars of the reel. (count = 1 quaver. 8 quavers per bar).

Count

1	Step on right foot
2	
3	Cross left foot over in front of right foot and step
4	
5	Step on right foot in situ
6	
7	Hold position (pause)
8	
1	Step on left foot.
2	

3   Cross right foot over in front of left foot and step.

4

5   Step on left foot in situ.

6

7   Hold position (pause).

A full step using this pattern might be:

Movement Pattern x 3 + finish = eight bars.

A variation of the previous movement is the following:

<u>Count</u>

1   Cross right foot in front of left foot, stepping on to both feet simultaneously.

2

3   Kick right foot forward, hopping on left foot at same time.

4

5   Move right foot back parallel to left foot and step on right foot.

6

7   Pause

8

A full step using this movement pattern could be:

Bar

1   Dance pattern off right foot (as above)

2   Dance pattern off left foot (mirror image of above)

3   Dance pattern off right foot

4   *Timeáil* x 2

5   Dance pattern off left foot

6   Dance pattern off right foot

7-8 Dance Finish

Some steps make use of a sidestep motif which involves moving right-wards or leftwards as directed. When right foot is leading, the dancer moves to the right and vice versa. A typical movement using the sidestep pattern is the following:

Begin with feet side by side.

Count

1	Right foot step to right and slightly forward.
2	
3	Bring left foot to a position stepping slightly behind right heel.
4	
5	Cross right foot in front of left and step onto right foot.
6	
7	Step on left foot in situ.
8	

A full step using this movement could be:

Bar

1–3	Dance above pattern 3 times thus moving rightwards each time.
4	*Timeáil* x 2
5–6	Dance mirror image of above pattern twice, thus moving left-wards each time.
7–8	Dance Finish.

The Northern Style

The northern style resembles the Connemara style in many ways. Firstly it is transmitted outside the context of a formal teaching situation. Secondly, the dancer develops his or her own repertoire of steps from the step elements and dance movements in the local area. The main foot position is, similarly, akin to normal walking movement and again the steps are not doubled. Finally, and most distinctively, it features prominently a form of heel-and-toe stepping which distinguishes both these styles from the southern tradition which rarely uses the heel in its step patterns. I would include in this style dancers I have recorded from Donegal, Fermanagh, Tyrone, Cavan, Meath and Sligo. Further fieldwork will no doubt add to the present sum of knowledge of traditional dance in the region of the country north of a line drawn from Galway to Drogheda.

Note: The Irish Folklore Commission

THE IRISH FOLKLORE Commission was established in 1935 and undertook the collecting, classifying, study and exposition of all aspects of Irish folk tradition. Under the auspices of the Commission, full-time and part-time collectors were employed to document folklore in every county in Ireland, and their collections, in the form of manuscript, sound recording, photographs, drawings and film, were deposited in the archives of the Commission, then based in St Stephen's Green, Dublin.

The Department of Irish Folklore is the immediate successor to the Commission, which was disbanded in 1971, and its staff and holdings were transferred to University College, Dublin.

Séamus Ennis worked as full-time collector from 1942 until 1947, concentrating on the collection of traditional music and songs. He worked in west Munster, Galway, Mayo, Cavan, Donegal and the Scottish Gaeltacht.

Seosamh Ó Dálaigh (Joe Daly) worked as a full-time collector from 1936 until 1951. He did most of his work in the Dingle peninsula and also worked in north Kerry, west Limerick, west Tipperary, west Cork and the Decies area of County Waterford.

Michael J. Murphy started working as a full-time collector for the Commission in 1949 and continued this work for the Department of Irish Folklore until his retirement in 1983. He collected in Counties Antrim, Down, Armagh, Tyrone, Fermanagh, Derry, Louth, Sligo and Cavan.

James G. (Jim) Delaney started work as a full-time collector in 1954 with the Irish Folklore Commission and continued working in this capacity with the Department of Irish Folklore. He collected in the midlands, in County Leitrim and in County Wexford.

Nioclás Breathnach worked as a full-time collector in County Waterford from 1935 until 1937.

P.J. Gaynor worked as a part-time collector for the Irish Folklore Commission, primarily in in Counties Meath and Cavan, and he also collected folklore in Counties Monaghan, Westmeath, Louth, Leitrim and Down. He worked as a collector from 1941 until 1958.

Bibliography

Ár Rinncidhe Foirne. Leabhair 1, 2, 3. Dublin: An Coimisiún le Rincí Gaelacha, 1995.

Breathnach, Breandán. Ceol Rince na hÉireann II. Dublin: Oifig an tSoláthair, 1976.

Breathnach, Breandán. Dancing in Ireland. Miltown Malbay, Co. Clare: Dal gCais Publications, 1983.

Burke, Stephen. Set Dances for Fun. Leo Publications, 1994

Carleton, William. The Poor Scholar. Dublin: James Duffy and Co. Ltd, n.d.

Carney, James D., ed. Poems on the Butlers of Ormond, Cahir and Dunboyne. Dublin: Dublin Institute for Advanced Studies, 1945.

Carolan, Nicholas. A Harvest Saved. Cork: Ossian Publications, 1997.

Connolly S.J. Priests and People in Pre-Famine Ireland. Dublin: Gill and Macmillan, 1982.

Croker, Thomas Crofton. Legends of the Lakes. London: John Ebers, 1829.

Cullinane, Dr John P. Aspects of the History of Irish Céilí Dancing, 1897–1997. Cork: Published by the author, 1998.

Cullinane, Dr John P. Aspects of the History of Irish Dancing. Cork: Published by the author, 1987.

Cullinane, Dr John P. Further Aspects of the History of Irish Dancing. Cork: Published by the author, 1990.

Cullinane, Dr John P. Irish Dancing Costumes. Cork: Published by the author, 1996.

Danaher, Kevin. The Year in Ireland. Cork: The Mercier Press, 1972.

Dean-Smith, Margaret, ed. Playford's English Dancing Master, 1651. London: Schott, 1957.

Dineley, Thomas. Voyage Through the Kingdom of Ireland in the Year 1861. Dublin: M.H.Gill, 1870.

175

Emmerson, George S. *A Social History of Scottish Dance*. Montreal and London: McGill – Queen's University Press, 1972

Fenton, Seamus. *It All Happened*. Dublin: M.H. Gill, 1948.

Flett, Joan. *Social Dancing in England from the 17th Century*. London: Vaughan Williams Memorial Library Leaflet No. 18, n.d.

Flett, J.F. and T.M. *Traditional Dancing in Scotland*. London: Routledge and Kegan Paul, 1964.

Franks, A.H. *Social Dance, A Short History*. London: Routledge and Kegan Paul, 1963.

Gilbert, J. T., ed. *A Jacobite Narrative of the War in Ireland, 1688–1691*. Shannon, Co. Clare: Irish University Press, 1971.

Hamilton, Frederick Spencer. *The Days Before Yesterday*. London: Hodder and Stoughton, 1920.

Hammond, William. *Call the Set*. Cork: Cork Folk Publications, 1988.

Hammond, William. *Call the Set No. 2*. Cork: Cork Folk Publications, 1988.

Head, Richard. *The Western Wonder*, 1670.

Hedderman, B.N. *Glimpses of My Life in Aran*. Bristol: John Wright, 1917.

Kane, Pat. *Céilí Night with Pat Kane*. West o' Clare Productions, 1995.

Kennedy, Patrick. "Irish Dancing Fifty Years Ago", *Dublin University Magazine*, vol. LX11.

Logan, Patrick. *Fair Day*. Belfast: Appletree Press, 1986.

Lynch, Larry. *Set Dances of Ireland: Tradition and Evolution*. Miltown Malbay, Co. Clare: Séadna Books, in collaboration with Dal gCais Publications, 1989.

Mac Lochlainn, Alf. "Gael and Peasant", in D.J. Casey and R.E. Rhodes, eds., *Views of the Irish Peasantry 1800–1916*. Hamden, Conn.: Archon Books, 1977.

McLysaght, Edward. *Irish Life in the Seventeenth Century*. London: Longmans, 1939.

Mac Mahon, Bryan. *The Vanishing Ireland*. Dublin: O'Brien Press, 1954.

McNamee, Peter, ed. *Traditional Music: Whose Music?* Belfast: The Institute of Irish Studies, Queen's University of Belfast, 1991.

Mac Néill, Máire. *The Festival of Lughnasa*. Oxford: Oxford University Press, 1962.

Maxwell, William Hamilton. *Wild Sports of the West*. London: E.P. Publishing, 1973; first published 1850.

Moylan, Terry. *Irish Dances*. Dublin: Na Píobairí Uilleann, 1984.

Moylan, Terry. *The Piper's Set and Other Dances*. Dublin: Na Píobairí Uilleann, 1985.

Moylan, Terry. *The Quadrille and Other Sets*. Dublin: Na Píobairí Uilleann, 1988.

Murphy, Pat. *Toss the Feathers*. Cork: Mercier Press, 1995.

Ní Mhurchú, Eibhlín. *Ceol agus Rince Mo Cheantair Dúchais ó 1800–1880*. Baile an Fheirtéaraigh, Co. Chiarraí: Oidhreacht Chorca Dhuibhne, 1990.

Nichols, John. *The Progresses and Public Processions of Queen Elizabeth*, vol. 3. London: John Nichols and Son, 1823.

O'Brien, Flann. *The Poor Mouth*. London: Hart-Davies, 1973.

O'Doherty, Eileen. *Set Left – Set Right*. Dublin: Na Píobairí Uilleann, 1989.

O'Doherty, Eileen. *The Walking Polka*. Dublin: Na Píobairí Uilleann, 1995.

BIBLIOGRAPHY

O'Keefe, J.G., and Art O'Brien. A *Handbook of Irish Dances*. Dublin: O'Donoghue & Co., 1902.

O'Neill, Capt. Francis. *Irish Folk Music: A Fascinating Hobby*. Wakefield: EP Publishing, 1973; reprint of Chicago: Regan Printing House, 1910.

O'Neill, Capt. Francis. *Irish Minstrels and Musicians*. Cork: Mercier, 1987; reprint of the original Chicago edition of 1913, with a new introduction by Brendán Breathnach.

O'Rafferty, Peadar. *The Irish Folk Dance Book I*. London: Paterson, 1934.

O'Rafferty, Peadar. *The Irish Folk Dance Book II*. London: Paterson, 1950.

Ó Súilleabháin, Muiris. *Twenty Years A-growing*. London: The World's Classics, Oxford University Press, 1972.

Orpen, Grace. *Dances of Donegal*. London: D.M. Wilkie, 1931.

Petrie, George. *Ancient Music of Ireland*. Dublin, 1855.

Quinn, Tom. *Irish Dancing*. Glasgow: HarperCollins, 1997.

Richardson, P.J.S. *The Social Dances of the Nineteenth Century*. London: Herbert Jenkins, 1960.

Robb, Martha. *Irish Dancing Costume*. Dublin: Country House, 1998.

Roche, F. *A Collection of Irish Airs, Marches And Dance Tunes*. Dublin: Pigott, 1911.

Rumpf, E., and Hepburn, A.C. *Nationalism and Socialism in Twentieth Century Ireland*. Liverpool: Liverpool University Press, 1977.

Ryan, W.P. *The Pope's Green Island*. London: J. Nisbet, 1912.

Sachs, Curt. *World History of the Dance*. New York: W.W. Norton, 1963.

Scott, Edward. *Dancing as an Art and Pastime*. London: G. Bell, 1892.

Sheehan, J.J. *A Guide to Irish Dancing*. Dublin & New York: John Denvir, 1902.

Tubridy, Michael. *A Selection of Irish Traditional Step Dances*. Dublin: Brooks Academy, 1998.

Walker, Joseph C. *Historical Memories of the Irish Bards*. London: T. Payne and Son, 1786.

Wilde, Sir William. *Irish Popular Superstitions*. Dublin: Irish Academic Press, 1979; first published in Dublin in 1852.

Young, Arthur. *Arthur Young's Tour in Ireland (1776–1779)*. London: G. Bell, 1892.

Index